The Stranger in Medallion Loafers:

Adventures of Allen and Juan

Austin B. Tucker

The Stranger in Medallion Loafers:
Adventures of Allen and Juan

Published by TBCN Just For Kids

ISBN 13: 978-1-942513-79-7

In this work "Dr. Woychuck" the camp director, is a real person and executive director of Scripture Memory Fellowship. Some of the artwork uses living models with permission. Most place names are real, but the story in the book is a work of fiction. The other characters, places, and incidents named and portrayed herein are fictitious or used in a fictitious manner, and any resemblance to the names, character, or history of any other person living or dead is coincidental and unintentional. Product names used herein are not an endorsement of this work by product name owners nor the products by the author or publisher.

To Chase and Erin and Allie,
my grandchildren,
and to all teens and preteens
who enjoy an adventure story.

CONTENTS

Chapter One
The Stranger in Medallion Loafers

On a hot August afternoon fifteen-year-old Allen, and Juan, his fourteen-year-old friend and next-door neighbor were tossing a football back and forth on the high school field. Allen noticed a man who seemed out of place. He came on the school grounds from the street, wearing a gray sweat suit and carrying a basketball under his arm. Allen noticed also he was wearing polished dress loafers. Allen kept an eye on the stranger who made one lap casually around the cinder track. Then halfway around for lap two, he ducked behind the corner of the school gymnasium, basketball still under his arm. "Did you see that dude?" Allen asked his younger buddy. "Something's strange here!"

"Yes, whoever went to exercise on the cinders wearing fancy dress shoes and carrying a basketball? Let's follow him and see what he is up to. He can't get in the gym to shoot baskets and should not be on the gym floor with street shoes anyway. Something is screwy about that guy! He carried that basketball and never dribbled it one time." The boys tried to be casual about it, tossing the football back and fourth as they followed him. Suddenly, glancing left and right, the stranger ducked into a stairway leading down to a service entrance. They saw the emergency exit held open by an arm of someone inside.

"That's the boiler room," said Allen. "No one will be there but the custodian."

""Yes," says Juan, "and we won't get in there unless he holds the door for us, too."

"That's not likely!" said Allen.

"Look!" said Juan, "That transom behind the shrubbery looks open a bit." The boys tried it and found it swung up easily and quietly. Outside, the window was almost ground level, but it opened over a lower floor about six feet below them. Juan did not hesitate to slip in and drop silently to the floor. Allen stowed the football in a shrub and soon followed, his heart pounding. On the floor with Juan, he looked up at the window just out of reach and gestured for his smaller friend to stand on his cupped hands so he could lift him up to the window to close it behind them.

When that was done, they slinked in the shadows toward the voices of the two men. Still, they could not hear what they were saying, so they risked edging a bit closer. Then they saw the two men, their backs turned. The men were giving their attention to the big boiler that circulates water for warming the building in winter. So far, the boys were undetected. Do they dare try to tiptoe close enough to hear what is being said?

When they did get close enough to hear, the custodian was talking. Allen whispered, "That's not English."

"Not Spanish either," whispered Juan. The man in the tan dress loafers was mostly listening. One thing needed no translation. The custodian made an expansive gesture with both arms thrown up and back as he almost shouted, "Ka-boom!" followed by a sinister laugh. Juan whispered, "That needs no translation!"

The custodian talked a bit more to the man in fancy loafers, who suddenly commanded, "Speak English! Always speak only English!"

They watched as the stranger peeled open his basketball as if it had a zipper on it. He took out a plastic bag and began to knead a gray putty-like substance. He climbed up a stepladder already in place against the huge boiler. He spread out the putty-like substance to the shape of a family-size pizza and stuck it to the top of the boiler. Then he pulled from his pocket something that resembled a fountain pen and pressed it into the clay. Then he smoothed it out again. He was quietly explaining something to the custodian.

Allen looked at Juan, raised his eyebrows, eyes open wide and mouthed one word: "Bomb!"

The bossy one gave some more orders to the custodian, which the boys could not hear. Then the two men exited the boiler room one at a time through the same door the bossy one had entered. The boys saw the one in the gray sweat suit casually walk back toward the cinder track from which he came. They waited in silent tension a few long minutes and decided the custodian went on in the other direction.

The sun was slipping behind the pine and oak forest next to the school, and the boys were eager to get out and head for home. Allen said, "Let me help you up to the window; then you can help me out."

"First," said Juan, "we need to get a sample of that plastic explosive!" Quickly he headed for the boiler and found the stepladder stowed in the near-by corner. Allen held the ladder while Juan hurried up to the top where they had seen the "clay pizza" spread. He dug off a piece the size of a large marble and put it in his pocket, smoothing out the place where it was taken. He hurried down the ladder. They carefully replaced the ladder where the custodian had stowed it. "We could go out the exit door," Juan ventured.

"Not me!" protested Allen. "It's a noisy door and someone may see us." He headed for the window where they entered. Juan followed right behind him.

Allen helped Juan up to the window, where he quickly opened the transom and made his exit. He looked past the shrubbery left and right and then beckoned his friend to follow.

Allen looked around for a box that might give him the extra reach he needed and finally found one that would work. When he had his grip on the opening, he used his last toehold to the box to push it away from the window. He didn't want to leave any obvious sign that anyone had come and gone this way. Juan helped pull him out. Then they once again pushed the transom back to closed position.

Allen retrieved his football, and they headed for home at a fast walk, guessing what that pair was up to. They agreed that they were up to no good. They agreed that a bomb was involved. They agreed that they needed to tell the police or someone in authority. Why would anyone want to blow up the school's boiler? That was still a mystery.

Chapter Two
Starting with a Bang

Gathering darkness replaced the long summer evening as the boys got in sight of home, walking fast and jogging and walking again the few blocks from the school to their homes next door to each other. The boys agreed to get together after supper before they tell either parent what they had seen. After supper, Allen chimed Juan's cell phone and told him he was ready to come over. When he found Juan, he was in his backyard, already set up with an experiment.

"This is the plastic explosive, if our guess is right," Juan said, holding up the malleable ball from his pocket a moment and returning it there. "I will keep it in my pocket for now. I dug out a couple of firecrackers left over from the Fourth of July."

Juan led Allen to the end of a wire in the middle of his backyard. He lifted an empty tomato soup can to reveal a small firecracker wired and taped. Together the boys went back to the other end of the wire, where Juan had wrapped one strand of the wire to the negative pole of a dry cell battery. The other wire was stripped and ready to complete the circuit. "I have wired the firecracker so that a spark will jump and ignite it when I close the circuit. Ready to try it?"

"I'm ready!" said Allen.

"You want to do the honors?" asked Juan.

"You go ahead," said Allen.

"Three, two, one, zero!" said Juan and touched the bare wire to the battery's wire-spring pole. The firecracker popped and the soup can rose a respectable six or eight feet into the evening sky and fell back to the ground. The boys ran to check it out. The can was slightly warped and smelled of smoke but was otherwise unhurt.

"Now," said Juan, "we will see if we are really dealing with plastic explosives, such as C-4." He took the ball of plastic from his pocket and divided it into two small marble-sized balls. "Since we don't yet know for sure that it is explosive or how potent it might be if it is, we will test only a tiny sample." Then glancing at his friend, Juan said, "I opened the circuit at the battery, but you go check and make sure the wire is clear of the dry cell before I attach it to the explosive."

Allen ran to the battery end of the wire and verified that the electrical circuit was open. Juan pressed the sample of gray clay around the small firecracker and attached the wire with just a tiny gap between the bare ends. He taped it tightly with electrical tape. Then he put the explosive beneath the same tomato-soup can and added a plastic bucket over the can.

"Now, we want to be around the corner of the garage for this experiment," said Juan, as he led his friend back to the dry-cell end of the wire. "You do the honors, this time," he said to Allen.

Allen took the battery and wire and glanced once toward the plastic bucket over the experiment. Then, both boys safely around the corner of the garage, Allen counted down slowly. "Ten ... nine ... eight ... seven ... six ... five ... four ... three ... two ... one ... zero!" As soon as he touched the bare wire to the coiled pole of the dry-cell battery a loud blast shook the yard. They heard pieces of plastic and metal ricocheting off the garage and the house. A second or two later pieces of the experiment began to rain down in the back yard and maybe elsewhere.

"I'm ... I'm glad you didn't use all that wad of plastic!" Allen ventured. Then they cautiously began to search for pieces of their experiment in the near darkness of the backyard. They found a few scraps of various sizes, but decided they would need to search again in the daylight.

Just then, Allen's dad called from his back door beyond the hedge and pine trees. "Hey boys! What's all the racket?"

Both boys ran to give him a report. Inside Allen's house, they told the story of the stranger with the basketball at the high school. They told how they followed him into the boiler room where he met with the school custodian and how they watched in secret as he spread the pizza-sized clay on top of the school's boiler. They told how Juan took a sample of the plastic, which they just detonated to verify that it was an explosive.

"We need your help to contact the authorities," Allen's said. "We didn't know if anyone would believe us; it all sounds so unreal!" His mother was immediately on the phone with Juan's mother. "Juanita, you might want to come over and hear what our boys have been up to today! I'll meet you at the front door." When Juanita entered, Allen's mother asked, "Did you hear that loud bang in your back yard a few minutes ago?"

"Yes! What are those boys doing now?" she asked.

Allen's dad greeted his neighbor with a reassuring smile and a polite handshake. He summarized the story he had just heard from the boys. "I have a friend in the sheriff's department. He's a member of our church and will not mind if we call him at home even if he is not on duty this evening. He needs to hear the story from the boys and give us some guidance."

Deputy Newton

Deputy Newton was on duty and soon pulled into the driveway in his cruiser. He was welcomed into Allen's home and introduced to Juan's mother. He listened to the story with a few more details. He took notes and asked questions. "Do you know the custodian? What is his name? Who is your principal? Have you told anyone else any of this story? Could you recognize the stranger if you see him again? Can you describe him? "

The boys assured Deputy Newton that this was the first and only telling, and promised not to say a word to anyone but proper authorities. They answered all his questions, Allen doing most of the talking. Deputy Newton told all gathered, "I will talk to the sheriff tonight, but I'm sure he will want to involve the FBI."

The deputy knew that Allen was about to begin his sophomore year at Pine Hills High School and Juan was about to begin his freshman year. He knew also that Allen's mother is secretary at their church and his father is an independent insurance agent with his own office. He had met Juan also at church with his friend Allen. He added to his notebook as he learned that Juan's mother is a college student online, pursuing her masters' degree in Education and Science and hoping to become a Science teacher in a high school. Juan's father is a Marine fighter pilot, deployed on a carrier in the Persian Gulf at last report.

He noted also in his notebook that Juan is a bright kid, a true geek, with a wide range of academic interests, especially Science. Allen told him that Juan knows a lot of astronomy and is a math whiz, among other things. Both boys share an interest in cell phones and all things electronic–especially the latest gadget.

The deputy thanked the boys for reporting what they had seen and suspected, and again strictly admonished them to stay away from that boiler room from now on. "And be sure you talk to no one but the authorities about what you saw and heard."

He looked each boy in the eye and received that assurance. Deputy Newton turned to Allen's seventh grade sister Esther, who sat across the room in silence taking in every word. "Can I count on you also to keep this in confidence absolutely? None of this need go outside this room! Matters of national security may be at risk. "

The deputy glanced at each of the three parents in the room and added, "We are counting on your parents also to guard this confidence as serious police business. Talk to no one outside of authorities and then only those who have a need to know." The sense of solemnity in the room deepened.

Juanita had a question for the deputy. "My husband is deployed on an aircraft carrier in the Persian Gulf. We talk occasionally online and sometimes by telephone. We do not keep secrets from each other. Do you have a problem with me telling him what is happening?"

"Certainly, I do not stand between any man and his wife or children. That goes double for a man deployed in the service of our country. But you need to make sure that the telephone line is secure and that your husband knows that he places his family and his country in jeopardy if a word slips out of your boy's involvement in thwarting a terrorist plot. We do not know who the perpetrator is yet, but we can assume that he is a dangerous man, probably a terrorist. If he does not shirk to commit mass murder of innocent Americans, then no one in this room should doubt how he might try to take vengeance on anyone who stood in his way!

"I expect our sheriff will call in the Office of Homeland

Security or the FBI to help with this case. You can expect someone from a federal agency to call on you soon. Or they may want me to bring you in."

Allen asked, "You mean we might be placed under arrest?"

Chapter Three
Here Comes the FBI

By eight o'clock the next morning, an unmarked sedan was in Allen's driveway and a man and a woman were ringing the doorbell and introducing themselves with FBI badges.

Allen's dad invited them in and asked if he might call over his neighbors, Juan and his mother Juanita. The female agent said they preferred to interview each boy separately but would be glad for his mother to be present for Juan's interview. They wanted to know from Allen some of the same things the deputy had asked. Were there any distinguishing characteristics of the stranger? Allen mentioned how strange he thought it was that he was dressed in a gray sweat suit and carrying a basketball he never dribbled once. And especially how strange he looked in tan dress loafers in that exercise suit. "Did it appear to be a well-worn sweat suit or more like new?"

"Like he was wearing it for the first time," Allen answered, "and like he did not belong in it somehow."

"Think about those tan loafers: can you remember any distinguishing features?"

"I got a good, close look at the loafers when he walked past the window where we were hiding in the boiler room. They were expensive looking loafers that clicked on the sidewalk as he walked past our window. There was a band across the instep and some kind of medallion on the band."

Would you recognize them if you saw them again?"

"I believe I would recognize that medallion."

Agent Alicia

The male agent was doing most of the talking so far, but he turned to his partner at this time. She took her cue and asked Allen, "Do you have a computer with online connectivity?"

"I sure do! I'm online every day."

"Will you show it to me? You and I will do an Internet search for those loafers."

"Sure! It's in my room. Come with me." He looked at the other agent and at his father for a nod of approval and got it from both directions. Agent Alicia, as she called herself, set at Allen's computer keyboard and opened a search engine. She put in "Men's loafers" and got thousands of hits. "Expensive looking, you say?"

"Yes ma'am. And tan or light brown."

Agent Alicia narrowed her search to the first expensive brand of men's shoes in the alphabet that came to mind – "Armani." In a few seconds she was showing an assortment to Allen. "Do you see anything like them here?"

They scanned the catalog pages and found a few that resembled the suspect in various ways. They moved on to search Angelo brand. Allen gave her running commentary of what he remembered that was a bit different. He mentioned details about the medallion on the loafers several times. Agent Alicia did a different search with "Men's Loafers + Medallion + Tan" and soon had a rise from Allen.

"Look at that one!" Allen exclaimed. "Zero in on that one." She did. "That's it!" said Allen, "Except it was definitely tan and not black. There is the same medallion across the top of the foot."

"You're sure? 100%?"

"That's it!" Allen insisted.

Alicia clicked on the picture and soon had the details. "Wow!" she said, "Our suspect likes expensive slippers. That's nine hundred bucks a pair!" She sent a copy to the printer and the link to her email at the FBI office.

Back in the den, the other agent had used his laptop to pull up a list of suspects on the terrorist list. Adding "Medallion" did not narrow the list down any at all, but from Allen's description and narrative of the encounter he searched for Islamist radicals. He soon had a sizeable collection of mug shots and snapshots for Allen to look through. Some vaguely resembled the lean stranger, but none rang a bell.

"Anything else you remember?" As he asked, he reached into his inside coat pocket and pulled out his leather FBI badge holder and slipped two of his business cards out of the inside pocket, one for Allen and another for his parents.

Allen noticed for the first time that the agent was armed with a shoulder holster under his suit coat. The agent said "Call us anytime, if you remember anything more. Anything at all!"

Allen, thought he should add, "When you interview Juan, he will have a tiny sample of the plastic explosive, which he will be glad to turn over to you. " (He held up his hand with thumb and forefinger indicating the marble-sized sample.) "You probably won't need to ask him. In his back yard you can see what a sample the same size did to a soup can and a plastic bucket. Tell me Sir, why would anyone want to blow up the school's boiler?"

"We will be interested in finding that out also, and believe me, we will find out! Remember now, you have been helpful to us and to your country. Don't go and spoil it all by trying to play detective. These people are very dangerous. You need to leave police work to the professionals from now on. Understand?"

"Yes Sir. Yes Sir." Allen assured him.

While the agents were moving their car from Allen's home to the driveway of Juan's house next door, Allen called his friend and said, "The next person to ring your doorbell will be one of a pair of FBI agents. I told them you have a sample of the explosive you will be glad to turn over to them. They should be turning into your driveway now! We'll talk when they leave your place."

Later that day, the two boys got together. Allen learned that Juan's interview proceeded along very similar lines. The agents wanted Juan's independent report of what happened at the school and at home. They asked for any details that might help identify the stranger. They heard very little that Allen had not given them already.

Both boys heard the warning to leave detective work to the detectives. Still, they wished they could help.

Chapter Four
Wannabe Detectives

Early the next morning, the boys went together to the woods next to the schoolyard. They had been in those woods often and knew there was the remnant of someone's tree house. It was close enough to the campus to see much of what was going on there but still isolated enough to be unnoticed. Through the trees they could see much of the school ground with cinder track and a small set of bleachers. They had a clear view of the wing of the school building with the basement entrance. Juan had his Nikon digital camera with telephoto lens in case anything of interest came into view.

All morning they watched from their perch in the tree and talked about what had happened and what might be about to happen. "Do you think we have stumbled onto a terrorist plot? Why the school? And why so much plastic explosive to blow the top off the boiler? If it is full of water it won't be hot in the summertime. And if it blows up the whole boiler like

Austin B. Tucker

that little sample blew up the soup can and plastic bucket, it would do no more than flood the boiler room with cold water. Still, the authorities are thinking 'mass murder.'"

"Juan added, "That bomb could also blow up the ceiling of the boiler room and whatever is on the floor above!"

"The auditorium! That's what's above the boiler room!" Allen suddenly realized. "I wonder if they are planning on a surprise for opening assembly?"

His younger friend suggested, "That's two weeks away? They would not be putting the explosives in place so far in advance. Someone might discover the plot. This bomb is set for something soon!

At midday, they found someone climbing their tree and looked to see Esther, Allen's younger sister, coming up with a plastic bag held in her teeth. Seeing there was hardly room for one more on the perch where the boys were, she tossed her sack up and swung around the tree to another limb. "I made some cheese sandwiches and brought a couple of bottles of water for you guys," she said.

"How did you know where to find us?" Allen wondered out loud.

"Oh, it's not hard to figure you guys out!" And she added with a twinkle, "And you know I do have the advantage of woman's intuition."

Allen retorted, "Shouldn't you call that 'girl's intuition' in your case?"

A Fuel Truck

Just then Juan spoke: "Heads up! We have some activity on the campus." A small tanker truck rolled up slowly to the door of the boiler room entrance. The driver got out and put on his work gloves and went to the rear of the truck. In a few seconds he had attached a four-inch hose to a tap at the base of the tanker and rolled out about twenty feet of tubing. Someone was working with him from inside. Juan was clicking away with his telephoto lens.

Allen flipped out his cell phone and dialed the number of his FBI contact. He was soon connected to him and identified himself to the agent. "We are in the woods beside the high school. A tanker truck just drove up to the door where the boiler is located and appears to be off-loading gasoline or something into that boiler room."

"Yes sir! ... Yes sir! Yes sir!" ... No sir! We are not on the school grounds. We won't go anywhere near that truck or the boiler room! ... No sir! No SIR! We are staying away! I just thought you would want to know. You did say to let you know if we saw anything else. ... Yes sir! ... Yes sir!" Allen flipped his cellphone closed and off.

"He's afraid we are butting in. He thinks we are going to get into trouble. He says we could give away to the perpetrators that they are discovered." The three watched in silence as the tanker finished one tank and moved the hose over to the other. It seemed to take a long time for the tank to drain. Meanwhile, the driver seemed to be nervously trying to appear nonchalant about the whole matter. He looked this way and that and frequently at the hose and toward the boiler room door.

Juan spoke to Esther, "We are glad for the lunch sack, but you really need to slip down from the tree. Your white blouse will be like waving a flag of surrender if that truck driver glances this way one time. We are in camouflage tee shirts and will not be noticed unless he sees you first."

"Yes sir, yes sir," said Esther, "I see what you mean. I might could catch the truck coming out and get a license number or something to identify it."

"Please don't try to do that," said her brother. "We are already in trouble with the FBI. Thank you, but go home and stay clear of all of this. We have been warned that these are dangerous maniacs." Esther slipped down the tree and silently made her way to the street leading home.

Allen and Juan watched a while longer. When the truck was gone, everything on campus had settled into an unnerving calm. Soon the boys agreed it was time to vacate their place of surveillance and head for home.

As they walked, Juan suggested, "If that is high octane gasoline or some other fuel going into the boiler, you have a bomb that could take down the whole school and everyone in it!"

As they walked toward home, Deputy Newton pulled up beside them. "Hi, boys. Get in, and let me take you home." They got in and before they could tell what they had just seen, they learned from the deputy that he already knew all about it. "Boys, you have been a big help, but you have been warned to stay away from the school and told not to try to play detective. The FBI has that whole school under professional surveillance. We don't need amateurs, no matter how talented and well meaning. "

"Why would they build a bomb big enough to level the whole school and half the neighborhood?" asked Juan. "And why so far in advance of opening assembly?"

"There you go trying to play detective!" answered the deputy with as much kindness as he could manage in a business-like voice. "I'll tell you this much in strictest confidence on condition that you back off and leave police work to the professionals. There is a town-hall type forum with a couple of senators and some other public figures scheduled to use the high school auditorium tonight. There will be maybe a hundred fifty or two hundred local citizens in the auditorium just above that boiler room. That is probably the target. Now can you keep quiet about that? The FBI has already asked me to keep you guys out of their business. They think you might need to be placed in protective custody. ... I'm trying to keep you out of jail, but you must promise to keep away from that school! ... Understood?"

"Yes sir" both boys said with resignation.

"But won't they cancel the meeting for tonight?" Allen wanted to know.

"Please don't worry about that!" insisted the deputy. "We are on top of it, believe me!"

Juan said to Allen so that Deputy Newton could hear,

"I think he means, if they can get the fuel back out of the school they will go ahead with the public meeting and try to apprehend someone attempting to set off the bomb they will have defused." Then to the deputy he directed a veiled question. "I'll bet the FBI has already defused that bomb by removing the plastic explosive."

"Smart kid!" said Deputy Newton. "Yes, of course, thanks to information we got from you two, the FBI removed that C-4 last night and replaced it with modeling clay that looks about like it. We would like to round up the whole cell of terrorists if we can, but we won't use American lives as bait. Now can we agree not to talk about this any more? I could get in trouble for what I have already told you. But I will try to keep your parents posted on a need-to-know basis if you will promise to stay out of it!"

The boys were silent.

"Are we in agreement?" asked the deputy in his most business-like voice so far.

"Yes sir," came two reluctant replies. The deputy let them both out in front of the Allen's house. They both wondered what they would tell parents about their ride home.

Chapter Five
Private Drive – Keep Out!

Allen and Juan felt like exiles. They could not go near the school. They decided to ride their bicycles around the neighborhood away from the school. Soon a familiar rusty pickup truck rattled past them. "Hey! That's the custodian!" said Allen. "Wonder where he is going. He lives somewhere out this way!"

"Well, we could follow, and maybe we will find out," said Juan.

"Yes, and maybe we could find ourselves in big trouble with the FBI, " Allen countered. Juan was already pumping to follow the rusty truck. Allen reluctantly fell in behind him. It was a long, straight highway through town. Before the truck disappeared from view on the rural edge of the community, they saw it slow down and make a right turn. When they reached that place, it was an unnamed one-lane road into the piney woods.

Austin B. Tucker

A sign at the turnoff read "Private Drive. Keep Out!" Juan peddled past the drive, looking as far as he could see into the piney woods. He turned off into the rough brush of the woods about fifty yards past the private drive. He dropped his bicycle into the grass and scattered a double handful of pine straw and twigs over it. He looked back to see if Allen was going to follow or not. Allen was not as eager as his younger friend, but he was not going to abandon him to go it alone. He rolled his own bike over the shallow ditch and into the same brush. He followed Juan's example of hiding the shiny metal.

As they advanced stealthily into the pine thicket, the brush and briars gave way to a thick layer of pine straw under towering Longleaf Pine trees. They struggled to see what might lie ahead. They wanted to see without being seen. Making their way slowly, and for the most part silently, over the thick carpet of pine needles, they advanced parallel to the private drive the rusty pickup entered. In a few minutes they could see through the thicket a bit of the truck and something of a house just beyond it. Do they dare venture closer?

Juan barely slowed down. Allen wanted to hunker down or to retreat to the bicycles at the road. Juan crawled back to him and whispered, "You wait here and watch while I make my way around to the back and see what we can see."

Allen whispered back, "We are going to be in trouble! Let's get out of here."

Juan answered, "I think I need to look around. I'll be silent and unseen. You go back to the road if you think best." Then Juan slipped almost silently through the pines and occasional azalea bushes and was soon out of sight.

Allen watched and listened but heard nothing but his own heavy breathing. He suddenly remembered his cell phone in his hip pocket and pulled it out and turned it to "vibrate" instead of "ring." He hoped Juan had thought to do the same with his!

Under Arrest

A few long minutes passed with nothing more than the sound of birds in the trees and the muffled whine of an occasional truck's tires on the thoroughfare that seemed far behind them now. Then Allen sensed someone behind him. He started to turn his head but found the cold steel muzzle of a .38 caliber pistol against his cheek. Looking out of the corner of his eye, he met the gaze of a serious face with an index finger to his lips insisting on silence. Then the man, draped in camouflage fabric to match the piney woods, gestured with his pistol for Allen to follow him in silent retreat. Allen's heart sank to his toes while he prayed that this was one of the good guys and not one of the terrorists!

They made their way back out of view of the little shack. The man with the serious face flashed the badge of a state trooper and told Allen to keep silent. Meanwhile, he flipped open his own cell phone and pushed a button and at the same time, pushed an earpiece into one of his ears. "Number Two, this is One. Meet me at point Alpha to pick up a passenger." He kept the pistol in his hand as he directed Allen with a hand on one shoulder toward the highway near where the bikes were hidden.

"Who are you, and what are you doing sneaking around this place?" He demanded of Allen.

The frightened teen gave his name and said, "My friend and I saw the school custodian planting a bomb in the school boiler room. We have been trying to help the FBI and Deputy Newton keep an eye on this guy."

"Don't lie to me. That's against the law, and so is interfering with a police investigation. You and your friend could go to prison for years if you don't get yourselves killed first!"

"Oh, no sir, I wouldn't lie. It's the truth! I'm not lying! Deputy Newton and the FBI did tell us to stay away from the school and that's what we are doing. We just happened to see the custodian's pickup turn off the road ahead of us and decided to see where he lives."

"Just save it. You can tell the FBI." They stopped short of the highway in the heavy brush and waited. Soon a State Police car slowed down on the highway. The officer holstered his pistol and took Allen by the arm and strode out to meet his partner. "Two kids are about to blow our cover. Put this one in your car while I go back for the other one!" He opened the back door and roughly thrust Allen inside.

"Should I put cuffs on him?" asked Number Two.

"Do whatever you need to do," answered Number One, as he turned and rapidly waded back into the pine thicket.

Witness to Murder

Meanwhile, Juan had made his way around through the woods in back of the little shack just in time to hear the front door open and close again. His heart pounded with the fear that someone had seen him and was coming after him! He ducked flat in the bushes and soon saw two men walk around to the back of the shack. One of them was the custodian. Juan looked again in time to see them walk businesslike into the woods, the new character leading the way. Juan followed off-trail as near as his daring manner allowed. He wanted to stay out of sight yet keep them within his line of vision.

A minute after they disappeared, he heard the custodian protesting, "No! No!" followed by a single muffled gunshot. Juan decided it not wise to try to get closer. After what seemed like a long, silent wait, he saw the stranger returning

toward the shack. He was alone and carrying a shovel he did not have when they went out. The stranger was definitely not the man in the Medallion loafers, but he had the same olive skin and dark hair. His eyes roved left and right as he returned to the shack. He went inside for a minute or two. Juan was torn between running for the road and waiting to see what would happen next. Meanwhile, he edged his way back to where he could see the front side of the shack. The only door was in the front. He waited, but he didn't have to wait long. The stranger came out and put a gasoline can and the shovel in the back of the pickup. The can sounded quite empty as it hit the truck's floorboard. The stranger wasted no time slipping behind the wheel of the pickup and heading it up the private lane toward the highway.

Juan pulled out his cell phone and pushed Allen's number. Allen answered from the backseat of the State Police cruiser a mile or so away. Juan spoke as matter-of-factly as he could in this situation. "Allen, where are you? I think I just witnessed a murder! I think your custodian is dead! Call the police!"

Allen answered, "At the moment I am in a State Police cruiser under arrest! I'll tell the officer in the front seat!" About the same time, Juan saw the other officer striding toward him with a badge held in outstretched hand. That same no-nonsense stare was on his face.

Juan ran to meet him shouting, "I think I just witnessed a murder. The school custodian! I'm sure that guy in the pickup truck just shot him and buried him in the woods behind the house!"

Just then they both heard and felt a big *Whoof* from the shack behind Juan. He turned to see the shack in flames. Turning back to the man with the badge, Juan saw him on his cell phone and heard him telling his partner. "As soon as you can, corner that guy in the rusty pickup truck. Then we need a fire truck at this location – now! The shack is in full blaze consuming any evidence we might have collected! Tell them we will need a tanker truck and all the fire extinguishers they can bring. We are too far from a fire plug for this shack"

Suspect Arrest

Allen heard the officer in the front seat answer, "Our deputy friend is coming this way. I'm behind the pickup. We will have that truck cornered any minute." Then Allen saw the deputy's car coming over the hill with bubble lights ablaze. His own car sped up and turned on his siren closing on the pickup from behind. The oncoming deputy swerved across the highway to block the path of the pickup. He hit his siren as well. The pickup tried to dodge around but saw no opening. He skidded to a stop on the side of the highway and jumped out with his pistol drawn. The state trooper grabbed his shotgun standing on the dash rack and shouted to Allen, "Get down! Get down on the floorboard and stay *down*!"

The two law enforcement professionals took positions each behind a door of his cruiser and each shouted at the same time with guns aimed for the stranger to drop his gun and get down on his face. The stranger hesitated for a moment and then tried to break for the woods. Both officers fired. Allen could not resist looking up to see what was happening. It appeared both officers aimed for the legs to avoid the loss of the only suspect they had left. The state trooper shouted, "The next shot will blow your head off, if I don't see your gun tossed out this way now!" There was still a little hesitation, but the gun was soon held up in the air by the barrel and then tossed toward the highway. Both officers closed in on him cautiously. Now Allen felt he could safely watch the rest of the arrest. They soon had the man subdued and handcuffed behind his back. The deputy was on his shoulder mike calling for an ambulance and backup at the "same ten-twenty" as the fire truck.

As soon as the backup deputy's car came in view, Allen's officer jumped in his car and turned it around toward his partner and Juan at the custodian's shack. A growing column of black smoke rose over the pine thicket. He turned into the private lane and jumped out to open the back door for Allen. "I need you to watch for that fire truck you hear coming. Wave them into this lane and tell them it is a crime scene. Can you do that? A crime scene!"

"Yes Sir! I can do that gladly!" He would rather go and make sure his buddy Juan was safe, but he was glad to be again of help to the authorities. The state trooper jumped back into the car and went bouncing down the lane toward the blazing shack.

Soon the firefighters came over the hill. They came in the big fire truck with the fire chief's car blazing the trail. Close behind them was the tanker truck. Allen waved them into the private lane. When they arrived where Juan and the state policeman stood a short distance from the blazing shack, the officer told the fire chief this was not one they should allow to burn out. Officers need to search for evidence in that shack if possible. The professional firefighters soon had the blaze under control, but there was not much left of it to explore for any evidence.

Juan told his arresting officer. "I think I can show you where to find a new grave and the body of the high school custodian. It's in the woods on the other side of that shack." He led his arresting officer down the path into the area where he had seen two men go and one come back after a single gunshot. They were not long in finding fresh dirt under a sloppy covering of pine straw and limbs.

The state trooper returned to the shack with his young prisoner and reminded the Fire Chief they were working a crime scene. He asked if the Fire Chief could station a man at the suspected gravesite until the coroner could come and exhume an expected murder victim. He added, "I still have a juvenile prisoner to question in this case. I expect he will have a lot to tell us."

After talking to the FBI on his police radio, the officer turned to Juan and said tersely: "As of this moment you and your friend are under arrest at the request of the FBI. You are in deep trouble now!"

Chapter Six
Miracle Camp

Once again, Deputy Newton managed to keep the boys out of jail. He reasoned with the federal officer in charge that both boys were scheduled to go with him to a week of summer camp. They would be far out of town and away from involvement in the ongoing investigation. They would not even be allowed to have cell phones at camp. And after all, they both had been considerable help to authorities so far. He would vouch for the boys and their families.

Deputy Newton explained to the boys that this was their last chance to stay out of jail, and it may not be a sure thing at this date. Not only were the boys guilty of interfering with a criminal investigation, maybe a terrorist plot, but their own lives and their families could be in danger. As the murder of the custodian shows, the ringleader of this plot does not like to leave witnesses alive.

The one in charge of this investigation was the FBI agent who had interviewed Allen and Juan and given each his card. Perhaps of the same opinion with Deputy Newton and perhaps moved by other reasons of his own, he agreed to delay jailing the boys at least for the one week of camp. He wanted the boys to know, however, that they were in double trouble, first for interfering with an investigation, and then maybe needing protective custody. If the TV news or print media had any knowledge at all of teenaged boys being involved in the arrest, they would not rest until they had found both boys and exploited their story. Deputy Newton, the state police, and the federal officers all knew that reporters have 24-hour-daily monitors on the police frequency just waiting for a big story to break.

So far, no reporters had learned about the failed attempt to blow up the school auditorium filled with dignitaries from Congress and citizens of the community. Unfortunately, neither was any suspect sighted trying to detonate the bomb.

A Story from the Deputy

On the way to camp, the deputy and his two passengers stopped for hamburgers and fries. Sitting at their outside table, Deputy Newton cleared his throat and said, "I have a story to tell you." They both gave their silent attention. He continued.

"One day a couple of months ago, I was having a hamburger and fries in a place much like this one. It was evening just after dark I was eating alone inside. Suddenly there came into the restaurant a remarkably beautiful young lady. She was dressed more for the opera than for a hamburger joint. She wore a black dress low on the shoulders and with a neckline that emphasized her well-shaped figure. I tried not to stare, but everyone noticed her as she clicked on the tile floor with very high-heel shoes. I soon realized she was headed straight for me.

"She came to my table and sat down just as if we had planned to meet there. She called me by my first name like we were old friends. I was sure I didn't have any old friends who looked like her. She said, 'I saw you as I was driving by and just wanted to stop in and say "Hello" and "Good-bye."

"I was puzzled and wondered if I might recall ever meeting this young beauty anywhere at any time. She soon made herself at home, picking up one of my fries every now and then and dipping it into my ketchup. I offered to buy her a hamburger. She shook her head and kept talking.

"She inquired about my wife and children and how my work was going. Small talk. I tried to answer her without telling her anything. Meanwhile, I searched my mind for any scrap of memory of ever meeting this beautiful young lady before. It occurred to me that it might be a joke of some of the guys I work with. Some of them do like to play jokes when work is slow. So I tried to play along.

"After a while, she said 'Well, it's time to say goodbye.' She stood and picked up her little clutch of a purse. She opened it up and pulled out a small .38 caliber Beretta and pointed it at my chest as she stood there on those spike heels. I was dumfounded! Then without another word, she pumped two shots right into my heart. And I never knew who killed me or why!"

The boys had been hanging on every word; now both let out a groan. They didn't know whether to laugh or douse him with a root beer. They both chose to show restraint. Deputy Newton maintained a straight face through it all.

Method in this Madness

Finally, Allen ventured. "You made up that story for a reason. Why? I think you had more reason than just to play a joke."

"You are right," said the deputy. "I need you boys to learn to play a role. Use your imagination. You are going to camp. You know that you are strictly forbidden by your parents and by the officers of the law to utter one word about what you know of this murder case or the attempted mass murder at the school. If word leaks out from any source, there will be TV cameras and news reporters crawling all over the camp to get your picture and your story. If they succeed, you and your families may have to go into the witness protection program. You will be moved far from your home, your school, your church and from anyone who knows you. You will be given new names and new identities. Your parents will have to start over in new careers. You will never be able to visit relatives even at Christmas time. You won't even be able to write them or call them on the phone. It's not a happy scenario.

"As you probably realize, what you have witnessed in the last few days is fantastic. Hollywood could hardly make up fiction as fabled as this truth. You could use a story such as I just told you to convince people that you make up fantastic stories. Your life could depend on it and the lives of everyone you love. Do you think you could play that role?

"Wouldn't that be lying?" asked Juan. "Wouldn't it be living a lie?"

Deputy Newton answered, "If you have to go into the witness protection program, your very life will depend on you playing a role like an actor on a stage. You won't be called *Juan* ever again or *Allen*. And your families will be in the same jeopardy. Of course, each family will go into a different distant state or possibly even a foreign country. Going together would make it easier for someone to trace you. You will have to say goodbye to each other and your friendship—and every friendship you have now. This is serious business. This is life and death business!"

At Camp

The boys were somber and thoughtful as they rode through Northwest Louisiana to Bienville Parish and to "Miracle Camp." When they registered at the camp, Allen looked at Juan and wondered how long they would be able to use their given names. Would they soon have to give up their very identity because of those killers? Meanwhile, the boys were glad they were assigned to the same cabin and relieved that Deputy Newton was assigned to be their cabin counselor.

A couple of hours behind them, Allen's dad came with Esther and three other girls from their church. Two of the four girls were teens and two pre-teens. They would camp in cabins on the other side of the lake from the boys. Allen's dad would stay for supper and then drive home.

The campers spent the rest of the afternoon exploring the recreation opportunities, paddleboats on the lake, canoes, and rowboats. Of course, life vests required on the lake reminded the boys that precautions are wise; this world can still be loaded with danger. They saw basketball and volleyball courts, shuffleboard and miniature golf and even a rock-climbing wall. There was a swimming pool with more cautions and rules for safe use posted there, too. Life could still be lived with excitement if one was not too reckless about the rules.

As the sun began to reach down to the tip of the tall pines, the dinner bell rang. After a hearty meal and some introductions, the camp director, Dr. Woychuk, made some announcements about the evening schedule. Before the evening service, the camp bell would ring for quiet time. Everyone should be ready to get alone with his or her Bible and have a time of private prayer and Bible reading. He suggested a good verse for meditation might be Psalm 46:10. "Be still and know that I am God." There is plenty of activity at camp, but we need to withdraw and listen for the 'still small voice' of God. He suggested if we do, we might expect to hear from heaven. He suggested that God had planned this place for them with eternal values in view. It would be a shame to come here and go away without every hearing from the Lord.

Juan and Allen looked at each other and knew that it would not be asking too much for them to get apart from each other for about twenty minutes. They would be back together and able to sit together in the evening service. After that, they could spend their nights together in the same cabin. This was going to be a great week!

Allen had been to camp before. He knew the routine. A few minutes before quiet time he took his Bible and found a bench out under the pine trees with a good view of the lake in the sunset. The simmering water reflected the evening sky with colors of purple and rose. When the bell rang to signal quiet time, he turned to the middle of his Bible and found Psalms. He read Psalm 1 and Psalm 23 and scanned some others. Then he came to Psalm 46 and found verse 10. "Be still and know that I am God."

He let out a deep sigh and thought; *I could do with a little quiet time! I need to be still, and I need to hear from God. My life has never ben so hectic as it is lately!* Then he silently prayed, *Lord, I'm listening if there is something you want to tell me this week.* Then he looked around for his friend Juan. He saw him on another bench not far up the hill.

Suddenly, he had the feeling that someone else was watching him. He looked slowly around and saw behind him Deputy Newton leaning against a tall pine where he could see both boys. They exchanged a timid wave. Then Allen turned his thoughts back to his Bible and read some more psalms until the bell rang again for evening worship. He joined Juan on the way to the chapel. Deputy Newton followed.

Evening Worship

They joined in the singing of hymns and choruses, led by their camp director, Dr. Woychuk. There was a time for volunteer personal testimonies and sharing of favorite Bible verses. Some read their verse; others quoted from memory. A group of college-aged young people, camp staff for the summer, sang a couple of special pieces. They were excellent!

Dr. Woychuk again welcomed everyone to Miracle Camp. He encouraged everyone to read the camp guide, especially the daily schedule and the rules and regulations for campers. Since this was a time and place for attention to spiritual values, the rules do not allow cell phones or transistor radios. There would be plenty of time for sports and recreation in the afternoons, but the evenings and mornings would be Bible-centered mostly.

The camp director read the story of the boy Samuel in the Temple of the Lord serving the aged priest Eli. Samuel heard his name called several times, and each time thought he was being summoned by Eli, the priest. The third time he came, Eli told him "Go, lie down, and if he calls you, you shall say, 'Speak, for your servant hears.' The Lord spoke to young Samuel that night and revealed himself to the young boy."

Dr. Woychuk urged the campers to tune the ears of their

spirit to hear if God chose to speak to them. It might not be an audible voice, but if they responded in submission, the Lord would make himself known. The preacher drilled the campers in saying aloud, "Speak, Lord, for your servant hears." He stressed that God most often speaks through the Bible.

When he was through explaining the Scripture and applying it to the campers, he explained that at camp, we do not sing an invitation hymn and ask people to come forward to join anything. But if anyone cared to stay behind and talk to a counselor about any spiritual matter, help would be available. After singing a couple of hymns more, the evening service was ended. It was time to go to cabins and end a long day with a good night's rest.

Chapter Seven
Trouble in Paradise

By the middle of the week, everyone was settled into the structured routine of camp life. The Reveille bugle sounded at 6:45 AM. Everyone got up, some slower than others, dressed and made up their bed. For many of them, that only required rolling up a sleeping bag or zipping it up flat on the bunk. There was not a lot of time to clean up the cabin with campers coming and going.

They hurried to make the time for the lakeside morning watch by 7:30. There they were encouraged to tune their hearts singing choruses and sacred songs *a cappella.* There was a time for "sentence prayers" from campers or adult leaders who might choose to volunteer to lead in a brief expression of praise to God or thanksgiving or petition. The beauty of this camp with lake and trees were mentioned often. After a brief meditation on a Bible passage led by the camp director, it was time for breakfast.

From the open-air area of Morning Watch, the whole gathering made their way by a narrow bridge across an inlet of the lake designated by signage, "Red Sea Passage." This pathway led to the dining hall. Breakfast waited. After a hearty meal of pancakes and sausage, juice and milk, and after a few administrative announcements, the assembly scattered again, some to finish preparing the cabin for inspection, others to a few minutes of Ping-Pong or some other table game before class time.

There were two classes in succession forty-five minutes each with a half-hour recess between the two. The classes convened in picnic-like tables under open-air canopies scattered under the trees of the campus. The adults had their own class in an air-conditioned conference room. After the classes, it was time to gather again in the chapel for a "morning rally" of about forty-five minutes before lunch.

After lunch, "rest period" is the order of the day. It would last about an hour, and it prepared bodies for an afternoon of recreation and water sports. The less energetic enjoyed visiting and just soaking in the beauty of the camp.

After supper and quiet time and evening service and cabin devotions another day ended with taps played on a bugle. Lights went out one by one all over the camp at 10:00 PM.

But for Allen and Juan and Deputy Newton, the day was not all peace and harmony.

Echoes of Trouble

Deputy Newton was often in touch with his office and other law officers by cell phone and text messages and email. He didn't tell the boys everything he knew, but as they heard he was in touch with developments in the investigation, they wanted all the news. Juan asked him what authorities were learning from the killer arrested. He told them that the prisoner, still under guard in the hospital where he was recovering from gunshot wounds, was a fountain of information. Much of it the deputy himself had not yet been told. But he knew that the killer's computer, recovered in the custodian's truck, was a treasure trove of data. The killer had inserted a thumb drive into the custodian's computer to download all his data before burning that computer in the shack fire. So they had data from two co-conspirators.

The big news was that word had somehow leaked out overnight that two teens were involved in uncovering both plots. These boys, so far unidentified, were known to have reported to the authorities the plot to set off a bomb in their high school. And then at least one of them was present when the custodian was murdered. So far, reporters had not discovered who they were. Otherwise, journalists would be camped out at their homes. Deputy Newton expected eager and enterprising reporters to soon narrow their search to the families involved.

"Does that mean we will have to move away and go into hiding?" Juan wanted to know.

"Not at this point," answered the deputy. "We are trying to avoid that by keeping investigation details away from the media. Of course, you surely know that their game is to find out somehow and spill it all out anyway. *The people's right to know,* you know. Some reporters believe that *the people's right to know* is part of the Freedom of the Press enshrined in the Constitution. In their minds it trumps your right to a secure life or to privacy. If you are news, you are fair game to the news merchants."

Allen wanted to know if there was any news from his parents. The deputy could tell them that his sheriff was posting a 24-hour-a-day watch between the two adjacent homes. "Of course, we don't want to wave a flag that these homes are under surveillance. That can attract the attention of neighbors who will naturally be interested in knowing why. It's a delicate balancing act."

He explained that the sheriff's office was prepared with the cooperation of the FBI and the state police to place guards inside the two homes if necessary provided the families were willing. Plans are underway to provide electronic surveillance of both properties.

"If necessary," said the deputy, "the police can provide guard dogs – maybe Doberman Pinschers – to guard the two homes." The sheriff had offered the two families to secure the premises with chain-link fences topped with barbwire. It did not take long for both families to say "No" to that, at least for now. They do not want their families to live in a compound like a prison.

The deputy tried to reassure the boys yet stress that this was a serious situation "The thing you need to know now is that the media hounds are trying to sniff out your trail and track you to wherever you may be found. They will come here to camp, if they learn who you are and where you are."

"So we should pray that they stay in the dark for our sake," offered Allen.

"Yes. Meanwhile the investigation must go on. We really need a lead on who 'Mr. A' is, and we need to find him. To that end, the FBI is sending two agents here to visit with you tomorrow. They want your help again. This time they need you to help them provide a composite drawing of the man. So far, you two boys are the only ones who can describe the bomber."

"When are they coming?" asked Juan.

"Probably tomorrow afternoon. I'm requesting that they bring your mothers with them or meet them here so that parents can be with you while you are questioned. Of course, I will be here for both of you, also."

Assurance

When Juan was alone with Allen, he confided in his friend. "Having to think about dying at our age is really heavy thinking. And the thing that makes it so heavy is I don't really know for sure if I will go to heaven when I die. Can anyone ever really be sure?"

Allen draped an arm on the near shoulder of his best

friend and let out a long sigh. He slowly inhaled. He weighed his words before speaking. Then he said, "Juan, the thought of dying young is a heavy thought for me, too. The terrorists may catch up with us with a bomb or a bullet. I don't know. I would much rather live a long life than die young, but whenever I die, I *know* that I will go to heaven. I don't wonder anymore about where I will spend eternity."

Juan was certainly not so sure. "How do you know? How can anyone be so sure?"

"There was a time when I was not sure," answered Allen, "but I remember the day when my doubts were settled. There are lots of verses in the Bible about assurance of salvation, but for me, when I went through a time of doubt last year, it was not a verse about assurance that made the day dawn for me. It was a couple of verses about how to be saved. I was memorizing my assignment in Youth Book 2 "Foundation of the Christian Life." Assignment 2. That book has a collection of verses under the tittle, "My Salvation Settled."

"But I just didn't know if mine was settled or not. I will never forget that afternoon; I was racking leaves and pine straw in our backyard. I had my memory book in hand with the rake, trying to learn my verses while I worked. All the time the title of that assignment was gnawing on my gut. *My Salvation Settled*! It didn't feel settled for me!

"Then all of a sudden the verses I was trying to memorize spoke to my heart. Romans 10:9-10 (NIV):

That if you confess with your mouth "Jesus is Lord," and believe in your heart that God raised him from the dead, you will be saved. For it is with your heart that you believe and are justified, and it is with your mouth that you confess and are saved."

"That shook me awake. I suddenly stopped raking and thought about what those verses were saying. *Well, have I confessed with my mouth "Jesus is Lord?"* I knew I had! *And have I believed in my heart that God raised him from the dead?* I certainly did and do! Then God's Word says I will be *saved!* All my doubts and questions vanished!

"Since then," Allen continued, as they paused in their stroll and turned to look each other in the eye, "Since then, I have found lots of verses that tell me I can be sure, but that day, when I needed assurance it was a verse about salvation that brought me assurance."

Juan spoke: "Well, I have confessed Jesus as my Lord and Savior, too. And I believe all the Good News about Jesus, too. Maybe I'm just afraid of dying so young."

Allen replied, "Well, that is something to be concerned about right now, but if Jesus died for us, we don't ever have to worry again about our home in heaven. That is settled in the death and resurrection of Jesus."

After cabin devotions and prayers, both boys slept soundly that night.

Chapter Eight
Putting a Face on "Mr. A"

Thursday dawned crisp and golden at camp. The daily routine was becoming comfortably predictable. Morning Watch by the lake followed by breakfast and cabin cleanup. Today the routine for the boys was changed a bit: the boys in their cabin had their turn with "K.P." – Kitchen Patrol! Allen and Juan followed the instructions of camp staff in clearing tables, sweeping floors, and other duties of cleanup.

On to classes they hurried, finding the teacher so interesting their minds were spared the thought of anyone searching for them. No reporters had found them yet -- much less any terrorist. Morning Rally was a lively time, and lunch was a delight. Rest time was really restful.

The Composite Sketch

Thursday afternoon, as the boys came from rest time to recreation time, Deputy Newton, their cabin counselor, called them aside. It seemed he had taken very little rest. He told the boys that an FBI agent had arrived. She was one of the two they knew already. She was waiting for them in the camp office. Both mothers were there also.

When they were all together, agent Alicia explained to the boys what she had already explained to the mothers. The boys would be interviewed independently. Two methods would be used to build a composite sketch. First, each boy would look at computer components of faces. They would start with a pair of ovals and build on it for a front view and a profile. They would place the eyes selected where they remembered them, the eyebrows, thick or thin or in between. The nose is important. Was the chin more square or round or even pointed? The hairline and hair color and style? Any facial hair – beard or mustache? What style? Both Juan and Allen, interviewed separately, made composite faces.

Then, the agent compared the two computer drawings. They were delighted to find they were remarkably similar. The FBI agent asked each of the two boys to look at a copy of both of the two renderings and decide, if possible, which one was closer to what they recall and how so. They each adjusted a few features on a clean-shaven face with black hair slicked straight back.

The expert remarked that this was a cagey operator they were dealing with. He might be expected to change his appearance when he moves around in public. On this trip, he wore no mustache or beard at all; he might have an entirely different appearance when he next surfaces.

There was still a lot unknown in their search. Who is this

terrorist? So far they don't have a name or even a nationality. They don't know what motivates him? It might be a big mistake to assume that he is an Islamic radical motivated by religion gone awry. Where is he now? How does he get from place to place? Does he have a sponsoring state or organization? If so, who? If not, where does he get his money? Why does he hate America so much? What is his grand objective? Where will he attack next? Who is helping him and supplying him with things like C-4 plastic explosives? He is not likely to bring these in from a foreign country – certainly not in an airliner.

"We have no fingerprints or even a footprint." Remarked Alicia, the FBI agent. "With so many surveillance cameras in public places, how does he manage to come and go without leaving so much as a shadow? Does he come through Mexico or Canada where it is easy to walk across our borders? Where does he come from and go back to?"

Leaving Camp

Camp was scheduled to close after the Sunday noon meal, but plans changed for the boys. On Sunday morning after breakfast, Deputy Newton informed them that the TV station had learned their names and had called their homes looking for them. They wanted to interview them for television news. The deputy reminded them: "You know the danger is multiplied for you and your families if they get your faces on TV. We don't know if they have discovered where you are right now, but we have posted guards at both houses and told the station they will not be welcome in either home. The FBI has arranged a safe house in town for both of you. We really hope this media frenzy will settle down in two or three days. Then maybe you can go back home and plan to start your new school year as normal kids."

"Meanwhile, if you can say your goodbyes after breakfast this morning, we won't wait for reporters and cameras to come rolling in the front gate of camp. We will head for town and the safe house. You will be very secure there."

On the way home, Juan asked the deputy, "What can you tell us about what the authorities learned from the man who killed the custodian?"

"I really don't know a lot," replied the deputy. "The FBI likes to keep the circle tight, and they are especially tight-lipped in this case. They have let the sheriff into their confidence a little bit. We know that the killer is out of the hospital and locked up in some federal facility waiting for a court appearance where he will be charged with murder. They will need Juan as a witness, if he ever goes to trial. The killer may plead guilty and go straight to a federal prison. In that case, they will not need Juan to appear in court.

"That would be better for you, Juan, but they will still need to interview you and take your statement and have you identify the killer in a police lineup."

"I'm ready to do that," answered Juan. "I'd rather not sit in a courtroom and let him see me! And I don't want any of his friends to see me finger him as the killer!"

Allen added, "And what about the guy who delivered the

tank of gasoline to the school?"

"We followed him back to his supply yard at the refinery," answered the deputy. "We took him into custody and questioned management at the refinery. Everyone pleaded ignorance, but the truck driver is still in custody. We may yet get some information out of him. Again, the FBI is in charge of that."

The trip home was uneventful. Deputy Newton led the way with Allen's parents and Juan's mother following in a van with the four girls. A short distance behind them, a local deputy from Bienville Parish trailed the two vehicles to the parish line and a bit beyond. A state police cruiser met them to escort them the rest of the way. At the church, the girls disbursed to their families. The boys went with Deputy Newton and the state police officer to a secluded estate on the southern edge of the city.

Parents and officers of the law questioned Allen's sister, Esther, to be sure that she was not talking to her girlfriends or anyone else about this case. Satisfied that she was bearing that burden alone, they urged her to continue to be mum. They told her that if the TV station or other reporters could not interview the boys they would be after her. They want someone with a face to say a few words they can broadcast to keep the story alive.

"We are more interested in keeping *you* alive," Agent Alicia told her, adding, "and the boys."

Chapter Nine

No Stars Tonight

It was the first night back home, after the week of camp and three days hiding in a "safe house." School was starting this week, and everyone wanted to try to get back to a measure of normal routine. The FBI had no news about "Mr. A" but did say they were following some leads generated by the arrested killer. The families involved convinced law enforcement to let them return home. That first night, Juan wanted to go outside. When his mother heard him open the back door, she called, "Where are you going?"

"I just want to walk outside a minute," he answered. I won't leave the yard; I won't be long." He knew his mother had already talked with Allen's parents and even with Juan's dad in the Persian Gulf. They had discussed being "prisoners" in their own home. They agreed to reject that as no way to live, if they could have a reasonable expectation of security. They knew that tonight a well-armed deputy was stationed in the back yard.

Juan stepped out on the screen porch and closed the door behind him. A very little light from a curtained window was all the illumination available. That glow did not seem to follow him out into the backyard. He could not see the deputy, but waved in the direction he expected him to be. Except for a distant streetlight around the bend of their street there was nothing to disrupt the darkness. His parents had talked about having a mercury vapor lamp installed in the back between Juan's house and Allen's. Nothing had yet been decided for sure; they might need to move away yet.

Juan looked up into a black sky. The moon was in the "new moon" phase. He always thought that should be called the "no moon" phase. He always liked this phase of the moon; it made the stars so much more visible. But there were no stars tonight; a warm front had pushed in a bank of low-hanging clouds to blot out moon and stars.

He remembered the brilliance of the night sky at camp where no city lights could diminish the dazzling array of the Milky Way. But here in his backyard tonight, it was dark and dreary. A chorus he learned at camp came to mind. It starts slowly and almost mournfully.

No stars tonight, No moonlight shining clear;
Dark clouds hov'ring, Not a ray of cheer,

Then the mood of the chorus brightens as the verse climbs all the way up the scale:

Only His promise, "I'll never forsake."

Conquers my fear, Conquers my fear.

(John E. Abnet. Copyright 1941 by Percy B. Crawford)

Juan remembered the promise of God's never-failing presence that strengthened his courage at camp. Joshua 1:5 "I will never leave you nor forsake you." Juan decided it was a good promise to claim at home as well.

Testing the Waters

Just then Juan's cell phone chimed in his pocket. He was not surprised at all that it was Allen. "Hey, Buddy! What are you doing?"

"Just testing my mom to see if she is going to let me out of her sight at night. I'm in the back yard. What about you?"

"I'm in the house," said Allen, "but Dad and I walked out a little while ago to take the deputy a mug of coffee and check on him. I think my folks are still nervous about me being out of their sight since being away at camp all week. And I think they are even more protective of Esther right now. Man! I had no idea what we were starting when we followed 'Mr. A' into that school basement!"

"But you would do it again, wouldn't you?" asked Juan.

"I probably would, but if I had known what we were getting into, I don't know. Maybe not."

Juan asked, "Have you had any more calls from the TV station?"

"None since the Sheriff talked to the station manager. The

station made it clear they will not be deterred from 'doing their job'. Now the newspaper is in on the hunt. They called and asked if they could get an interview, or even a statement. My dad told them politely that we need to be left alone, and that even that statement from him was not for the record. Officially, we are in the 'no comment' mode. He was polite but firm."

"That's about the way my mom handled them when they called her. We have not heard the last of reporters, I'm sure – radio and TV and newspapers."

"What are they saying about the Doberman Pinschers Deputy Newton talked about?" Juan asked.

Allen had not heard much, but he knew his mother did not want a dangerous dog in her house. She had suggested a more traditional housedog that could be trained to alert on any stranger coming near the house. No decision had been made. There was still the possibility both families would be put in the witness protection program and sent away from home to who knows where.

Juan said he had checked out the Doberman online and learned that they are not all so aggressive now as in earlier days. They are bred more for pets now in the USA than for military and guard duty. Still, he was not sure he wanted one in the house with him.

Small talk continued. The boys just wanted to visit. A month ago, it was common for either one to go over to the home of the other one for a visit even at night. Juan might spend the night at Allen's house and Allen with his younger neighbor. Last year they had camped out in a tent more than once in these very woods between the two back yards. They wondered if that time would ever come back.

Heads Up

Suddenly Juan heard the percussion of helicopter blades approaching low and fast. When the helicopter reached overhead it circled around the two properties and gained a little altitude. On a second pass, a searchlight from the whirlybird switched on and began to sweep the houses and the two yards. Juan could not hear his friend on the other cellphone, but he made himself heard to Allen. "Hey Buddy, you need to see this! Something's going down! I'm going to hang up. Come on out and see."

Just then the landline in Allen's house rang. His dad ran to pick it up. Caller ID told him it was the sheriff's office calling. Mr. Anderson called out to the family: "It's Deputy Newton calling." After a moment on the phone, Mr. Anderson said, "They're here now. It sounds like they are right overhead.

Now a floodlight is sweeping our property including our windows and doors. ... Sure, come on!"

When he hung up, he spun around and asked, "Is everyone inside? Where is Allen?" Esther had come into the den from her room in time to see Allen respond to Juan's call and bolt out the back door to see what was going on.

"Allen just went out back!" she answered.

"What's going on?" Allen's mother kept demanding.

"Tom Newton is on his way. He thinks they may have caught 'Mr. A' in our backyard. Reinforcements are on the way. He wants us all to stay inside and out of sight until they have searched the property." All the while he was running to the door to get Allen back inside. Soon Deputy Newton's car was in the front of the house and a few minutes later another squad car was in the driveway with red and blue lights flashing.

When things settled down, Deputy Newton came in and told the family what happened. An intruder penetrated the perimeter of the property from the back. He was making his way toward the house near the line between Juan's house and theirs.

Allen's mother interrupted. "Is it safe to call Juanita over now?

"Oh, Yes," answered the deputy. "She and Juan will want to hear this, too. The property is all clear now." It didn't take Allen long to speed dial Juan and tell him to bring his mom and come hear the news. And it didn't take those neighbors long to come over."

"You know, we have a guard posted. He's one of our deputies. He knows we really need to take any perpetrators alive to get information. Our guard has a Cherokee Indian blowgun and darts dipped in a quick-acting knockout potion. The deputy heard the intruder advancing through the woods in back and saw him in his night-vision scope. Instead of shooting him with his rifle, he dropped him with a well-aimed dart to the carotid artery on his neck. The intruder took two or thee steps and collapsed in a heap."

"The helicopter swooped in to see if he came alone. The first time they circled the property, infrared scopes were searching for anything warm enough to make an image. The only thing they picked up besides Juan and our deputy and his prisoner was the deputy's coffee cup with some hot coffee still in it. The second sweep with searchlight on was just to be extra cautious. We were listening on the police band to the helicopter and our deputy on the ground. That's when I headed this way and called you."

"Who did they catch?" Everyone was eager to know.

"The culprit is still groggy from the knockout dart," said Deputy Newton, "but our man has tentatively identified him as a photographer from the local TV station. He had a TV camera with a telephoto lens when he was arrested. It appears he was determined to be the first to get a picture of one of the boys. I don't think he got close enough to use his camera, but in any event we have confiscated everything he had on him."

With a chuckle, Deputy Newton continued, "When he

wakes up, he will find himself in our parish jail and deep, deep in trouble. His station will need to hire him a good lawyer. I'm sure he will be charged with trespassing, interfering with a police investigation, and possibly conspiracy to commit murder, since any information his station published would soon go viral all over the nation and likely inform our 'Mr. A' of who foiled his plot at the school and who witnessed the murder he probably ordered."

Juan ventured, "If you can find a law against stupidity, he could be charged with that, too."

Allen's dad wanted to know, "Are we officially calling him 'Mr. A' now?"

"Yes, I'll tell you about it tomorrow, but we had a meeting with Federal, State and Parish authorities to find what we know and don't know about this case. One of the things we agreed on is not to call the suspect, "Mr. Amico," That is a prominent family in Sicily; they might not appreciate the name smeared with the misdeeds of a terrorist. So from now until we have a real identity, he is 'Mr. A.'"

After social visiting for a while and setting a time tomorrow for the further briefing, the deputy said goodnight. He asked if he might exit by the backdoor so he could check with his night watchman, the deputy, once more before leaving.

Allen's parents and Juanita agreed that they were in good hands with the police who were watching over them day and night. And Allen reminded them that they have a Heavenly Father who also never slumbers.

Chapter Ten
The Man with No Shadow

The next afternoon, as planned, Deputy Newton visited Allen's house again. When he was in the den and seated, Juanita and Juan came in from next door. As coffee was served, Deputy Newton began.

"The main purpose of this meeting is to give you a briefing, as far as I am allowed, on the status of the investigation. The interagency task force has about a dozen officers from FBI, sheriff's department, state police and local police. The FBI is officially in charge. We have been meeting often in small groups, but yesterday we had a task force meeting to better coordinate our work. We need to know what each other knows.

Briefing the Families

"At this time, for reasons of their own, the FBI is not telling all they know. For instance, they were in charge of interrogating the killer of the school custodian. We don't know yet what they learned. I suspect they need to keep some cards close to the chest for security and for the ability to control the investigation.

"When the full task force met, we gathered in front of a couple of big ceramic whiteboards to do brainstorming. The facilitator began by writing across one of the boards, "What do we know about Mr. A?" Then on the board under that heading he listed what we know or mostly don't know so far. For example, Name? *Unknown.* Nationality? *Maybe the Middle East? Maybe not.* Residence? *Unknown.* Members of the interagency task force chimed in from time to time. Is he in the USA at the moment? *Unknown.* How does he come and go to enter the country and slip away again? *Unknown.*

"It is not likely he enters by standard airline. He would be on surveillance film. He seems to be too smart for that. And he could not bring C-4 or any explosives in by airlines. He could not even bring a weapon, and we assume that he does travel with a handgun, at least. But again, we just don't know.

"We discussed alternatives for his coming and going. We know that some aliens prefer to enter through Canada or Mexico. It's not very hard to cross our northern or southern borders. We explored the possibility that he might enter from our Atlantic or Pacific coasts. It's doubtful that he has access to a foreign navy to bring him by submarine or some such military operation. But again we don't know!

"On another part of the ceramic board we brainstormed whether or not he has associates in USA? Again, *Unknown.*

He is able to enlist confederates here and abroad such as the school custodian and the man who killed him. Does he have a sponsor here or abroad? *Unknown.* Is Mr. A really the kingpin or just an underling? There is so much we don't know!

"On another board we made a list headed *What we do know.* It is a short list. We know basically four things: One, he's a bold and cold-blooded killer. Two, he hates America and Americans, or so it seems. Three, he seems to like expensive shoes. He is probably well financed by some organization if not some foreign state. Or he may be from a family that is independently wealthy as was Osama Bin Laden. And four, we have a good composite sketch of his likeness and helpful details from the boys. We know how he walks with head erect, lean and lanky of stature, sure footed. He seems to have a bossy disposition This and other little details may one day help us arrest this man. More than half of what we know for sure, we know because of these two boys.

"I mentioned earlier, the FBI may know a little more from their interrogation of the man who murdered the custodian, but that's about all they are contributing to our corporate effort at this point. The big exception is that they found the killer's rental car not far from where he was arrested. He had the car stashed on a parking lot of a little strip mall. In the car was his laptop computer with a lot of information, it seems. I understand that it was mostly in a foreign language with a lot of code words and names."

Junior Detective

Allen raised his hand to pose a question: "Do we know where the rental car was rented?"

"Very good question!" answered Deputy Newton. "That's good thinking. And yes, the FBI traced that as soon as the vehicle was impounded. It came here from an airport car rental agency in Bradenton, Florida. That's on the Atlantic coast. He drove it from there to here, we are sure."

"But back to the laptop computer found in the rental car; there was a lot of helpful data in the memory, including some incriminating things retrieved from the disk drive that had been deleted. FBI translators and code breakers have been able to put together a picture from that computer and probably from interrogation of the killer. I am going to tell you what I know or have strong reason to surmise about this ring's plans for the USA. I stress the need to be absolutely closed mouthed about all you hear in this conversation. I am only able to tell this because most of it is unofficial.

"I don't know if the bad guys are able to do all they would like to do, but they have really big plans. From several sources including the killer's laptop and the thumb-drive copy of the data in the custodian's computer, and I suspect, some from interrogation of the captured killer, and from other sources, there is a whole basket of plots to do damage to our country and our people.

"For one thing, they aspire to destroy the US financial system. They would like to break the code of Wall Street computers. And 'Mr. A' seems to have a strategy for wrecking our whole transportation system. He has a team, (or I think he is still trying to enlist a team), to do that. They will destroy key bridges that link our nation east and west. They want to bring down bridges over two main divides in our Interstate highways. They will target bridges over the Mississippi River, such as Memphis, the I-30 corridor. And Interstate 10 at Baton Rouge and Port Allen are key targets. The bad guys want to shut down traffic at Natchez and Vicksburg, Mississippi. They also target alternative routes at Greenville's highway 82 and the bridges on I-155 at Dyersburg and I-57 at Cairo, Illinois. They are targeting the Highway 72 Bridge at Cape Giradeau and three interstate crossings at St. Louis. That's a big and bold plan.

Looking around at each face, he continued. "There is more to their grand plan to cut the USA in two. They plan to use high-powered rifles with tracer rounds on east and west commerce and communication. Another target will be rail lines at trestles. They can pull railroad spikes and cause a train wreck on the trestle or set bombs on oil tankers. They want to do the same to target gasoline transport trucks on rail and highway and storage facilities. It does not take an army to do a lot of damage with that plan.

"When law enforcement is shifted to cover one target, they can relocate to another. For example, they want to shut down Interstate-10 from east to west. It crosses lots of swampy territory in the gulf-coast states, making detour hardly possible. That is the case with Tallahassee and Pensacola, Florida, and at Biloxi and at Gulfport, Mississippi.

A cut in the Interstate-10 highway system east or west of Lake Charles, Louisiana and east or west of Houston, Texas will halt interstate commerce. We are skeptical that 'Mr. A', or whoever may be pulling his strings, has all the manpower available to do all the damage he aspires to do. Still our task is to make sure he does not succeed in any of it.

"While they are shutting down highway commerce, they also want to cut key rail lines east and west. They are targeting railroad trestles not only over the great river basin but especially through the "Great Divide" of the Rocky Mountains."

More Plots Brewing

The deputy paused to look around at each person for any response. No one was asking questions. Most faces showed a measure of shock. He continued with his report. "Another team will set forest fires wherever in the continent conditions are dry enough, especially when it is windy. They will use a homemade Molotov cocktail dropped from automobiles or private airplanes. They can do the same in populated areas when weather conditions dictate.

"Another very bold plot even targets Air Force bases such as Barksdale, near here. They want to infiltrate the bases on the ground and be ready to attack the flight line when bombers and fighters are on the ground. At the same time, they plan to set up rocket-propelled grenade launchers at highways to the south of the base perimeter and in the rural areas north of the runways to bring down B-59 bombers in takeoff or in final approach of landing. Frankly, I think such a plot has little chance of much success, but it does not take much success to strike a big blow to our military. If they get a strike team on base, they plan to attack storage facilities of petroleum supplies. And they may even target missile silos which you probably know have nuclear warheads. The FBI is bringing US Air Force operatives in on that part of the grand scheme.

They are planning an attack on the electrical supply system to put great cities in the dark and cripple us with the lack of everything electrical. They can take out transformer sites with little effort. They hope to start a chain reaction with one system throwing out the next.

Allen's mother circulated with the coffee pot to warm the cups of adults. Juanita helped with the pitcher of hot chocolate for the young people. Juan had a question: "You have not mentioned any plot to assassinate witnesses. Allen and I both feel like we have targets painted on our chests – or backs – or both!"

Deputy Newton nodded approval again. "You are correct again! We do not have proof yet, but we must assume that if the bad boys learn that you guys are the ones who short-circuited their plans, we have to assume they will try to strike back. And they will plan to leave no living witness to their crimes. That is a lesson we learn from the murder of the school custodian. He was a partner in crime with *Mr. A.* Now he is dead.

"While we are on this topic, I want to mention a matter we have left undecided. You accepted the risk of returning to your homes against FBI advice. We have greatly enhanced the electronic security systems in both homes and the property surrounding them. We have motion detectors inside and out, ultraviolent light, and a whole bank of monitors. We have 24-hour surveillance on the monitors from the sheriff's department right now. We won't be able to spare deputies day and night forever, of course. We have talked about adding trained guard dogs here at both homes. We can provide a pair of dogs -- perhaps Doberman Pinschers. They will be trained to alert on any intruder. Both families have so far resisted that idea."

Allan's dad thanked him and added, "We have not finally rejected the possibility of guard dogs. We are just reluctant to go there. We don't want the homes, ours or Juanita's, to be unwelcoming to friends and family who want to come and go. We don't want to become prisoners in our own homes."

"We are going to catch this guy, believe me," said the deputy. "

We have major resources devoted to the task. He seems to have the upper hand at the moment, but we will eventually cast a net over this man who seems to leave no footprints and to cast no shadow."

Chapter Eleven

The Big Surprise

The second week of school was almost over when the teacher in Juan's class interrupted the reading assignment with a puzzling set of instructions. "Class, do you remember how to salute? Put your books in your book bag, then we will stand together and review our drill on the proper military salute." They slowly complied with bagging books and zipping the bags. When they were all done, she asked the class to stand and salute. She coached them, "Fingers together, straight, not bent, hand in line with your wrist and forearm, elbow up so that the upper arm is horizontal with the floor. Look sharp," she insisted. "Stand erect at attention." Looking over the class, she made a couple of corrections with a couple of students who were less than enthusiastic. Then when she was satisfied, she reminded them, "When your salute is returned, drop that arm to your side sharply." She returned their salute as if she were in uniform.

"You may be wondering why this drill," she continued.

"We have a visitor in uniform who has entered the room at the back door. And I think I know who he is. Let's turn to face our visitor and give him a sharp salute!"

When the class turned, there stood a marine aviator in dress blue uniform. The class saluted him. He returned the courtesy. Then a very excited Juan broke and ran as he

shouted, "That's my dad!" He hung on the marine as they made their way toward the front for the major to accept the teacher's outstretched hand. The major said, "That was a nice welcome home. I hope you will forgive my interruption to your class."

"It is a great treat to have Juan's father visit the class," she answered. "The bell will ring any moment to end this week of school. We are all very pleased to meet you."

As if on cue, the bell did signal the end of class and the end of the second week of classes. The students made their way to the exits. Several of them came by to shake hands with the Marine aviator. After a brief visit with the teacher, Juan wanted to hurry his dad to see his best friend Allen. They found him waiting with his own dad in the carpool line. Together they rode the half-mile or so to their street and their homes side-by-side.

Time Flies

The days passed swiftly, especially for Juan and his parents. During the day, through each of the first ten days, Juan was in school restless to be out and spend time with his dad. Juanita tried to balance keeping up with her job and her own schooling. She was as restless as Juan to be home with Carlos.

The evenings and weekends were filled with catching up and spending time together. The major was always organized even at leisure. He budgeted time to spend with his son and his wife and for the three of them together. If they were going to have Carlos's favorite meal, they went grocery shopping together and selected three beefsteaks, potatoes for baking, and salad fixings. Carlos would fire up the charcoal grill and be in charge of the beef. Juanita tossed the salad and baked the potatoes. Juan helped with setting the table. Every evening meal had to be a special production with tablecloth, placemats and cloth napkins; the good silverware and stemware glasses came out of the top cabinet.

This was the pattern also when Allen's family had them

over for dinner or when they came over to eat with Juan's family as they did several time during the leave. When both families were together, the conversation often drifted to issues they shared in common. The parents especially wanted to talk about family security and safety. They all wanted to stay in the community if possible with church and school and friends. One evening together, Carlos revealed that his leave might be cut short by a transfer. Before leaving the carrier in the Persian Gulf, he had completed paperwork for a lateral transfer to Marine Corps Intelligence. He expected it to go through soon with his commander's support. Then he would be shipping out for about ten days or two weeks of orientation and training at Quantico, Virginia or maybe in California. Juan was almost shocked to get this news at the same moment as his neighbors.

Though the adults were having this conversation as if the children were not present at all, Juan stepped into the discussion. "Does that mean you may not have all your three-week leave?"

"That's right," said the major, "but a big compensation for that is that I hope to be assigned to the investigation of the terrorist who has dared to mess with our boys. I could be stationed at Barksdale Air Force Base and live here at home. Would that be Okay?"

"Wonderful!" exclaimed Juan with a generous bite of medium rib eye steak held high in the air on the end of his fork. "That would be ever more than wonderful!"

The New Assignment

As it turned out, Major Carlos received a phone call the next day from his commander on the carrier in the Persian Gulf. The major learned that he could expect the official transfer to come through in the next day or two. He would be going to Quantico, Virginia for about ten days of orientation in Marine Intelligence. Then he would be assigned as a liaison to work with the USAF at Barksdale. He would have a partner, probably also a major in Air Force intelligence. They would be equal partners. If his partner happens to be a Colonel, he knew the major would have no trouble working under his direction. Their assignment will be to find the terrorist or his superior who is allegedly planning attacks on Barksdale and other military bases.

Such staff and budget as they need will be provided. One more thing his commander wanted to be clear. "If this conflict over here heats up, I will want you back on board with your old team in your old squadron."

The lateral transfer came through as planned and the major packed his bag and went to Barksdale where a seat on an Air Force plane was reserved for him for the hop to Quantico.

Intelligence Duty

In two weeks, Major Carlos was back home with duty station officially at Barksdale. His counterpart in the air force was also a major. Major Trevor Washington had an office staff in place and files started. The first week back in Louisiana, Major Carlos and the USAF officer made trips to the Caribbean in civilian cloths and civilian aircraft looking for a lead on "Mr. A." They visited several airports, met other pilots and mechanics and showed the sketches of the wanted man.

With ample copies printed, Major Carlos would approach a mechanic or a line boy pumping gasoline: *¿Oye, Hermano ha visto usted a este hombre?* (Hey Brother, have you seen this man?) Most of them would glance at the sketch and shake the head *No.* Some might study it a few seconds and ask: *¿Quién es él?* (Who is he?)

It seemed an exercise in futility. But a few days later, Interpol, the international police agency, learned from their Caribbean eyes and ears about the two "flyboys" working with the FBI and asking around for information about a much-wanted fugitive. Interpol wanted a meeting for mutual benefit. Carlos arranged for the meeting in New Orleans, at Lakefront Airport the next day. Interpol would fly up from their Caribbean headquarters at Puerto Rico.

The next day was a Saturday and the boys were out of school. Majors Carlos and Trevor Washington of the Air Force flew the boys in a Lear Jet to New Orleans for the rendezvous with Interpol. They arrived at Lakeside Airport and taxied to an isolated station to await the Interpol plane. By prior arrangement, the Interpol agents came over to the BAFB jet with some glossy prints and a laptop computer for showing a few film clips.

Each boy viewed the glossy prints like a photo lineup. Each picked out their "Mr. A" independently from glossy prints and again from a video clip. Juan met with Interpol and Major Carlos in the back of the corporate jet while the other waited in the pilot's cabin. Juan selected "Mr. A" immediately. He swapped places with Allen who made the same selection with equal ease. "Mr. A " was not in disguise at all. He had the same slicked-back black hair, the erect, stiff walk, and he looked just like he did when he first appeared at their school. Allen ventured the opinion that if they could get a close-up of his footwear, it would likely be Medallion loafers!

The Interpol officers were most appreciative but non-committal to the boys. They promised to give their report to the two majors and the FBI agent who came with them. The boys didn't need to be told. They both knew that they had each hit a homerun this time at bat.

After the five agents had huddled a half-hour without the boys, everyone was in high spirits. They said their goodbyes, thanked the boys once more with handshakes all around and parted ways to their respective home bases.

As soon as they were airborne, Juan went forward to watch the pilots fly the big jet. His father explained to him a lot about radio navigation and cross-country flying. Major Trevor Washington, his teammate from the Air Force, was at the controls. Juan learned to set the frequency for an Omni-range radio signal that would guide them toward their home base. He saw on a map called a "Sectional Chart" how they can crosscheck their progress on course with the map and a compass.

Allen, in the passenger cabin, moved up to a seat beside FBI agent Alecia. He asked, "Do we now have a name for this guy we have been calling *Mr. A.*"

The friendly agent answered, "I don't see why you should not know; it will soon be online on our website and Interpol's. Interpol will issue what they call a *Red Alert*.

I hope we can get him on our Ten Most Wanted list and maybe on television. His real name is Amir Hussein Ra'd."

"So he is Muslim then," said Allen.

"He has a thoroughly Islamic name. His parents chose that. I personally don't think he is a devout Muslim. He may use jihad as an excuse for a deep hatred for America and Americans. From what Interpol told us, he is a common criminal in love with himself." The agent lapsed into silence and turned her attention to the passing countryside. The Lear Jet leveled off at cruising altitude. A few puffy white cumulous clouds slipped swiftly and silently under them in the smooth air.

Allen hoped to continue the quiz. "Why does he hate America if it is not driven by his religion?"

"That's one I would like to know," said the agent.

"You said, 'common criminal'; what criminal activity has he been into besides murder, attempted mass murder, and terrorism?"

Agent Alicia chuckled at the astute question. "It seems Interpol knows him mostly for drug smuggling, passing counterfeit American bills, and other crimes. You might remember the recent billion-dollar seizure of a whole shipload of heroin and other drugs bound for Europe. We think that Mr. Ra'd owned a piece of that action and then sold them all out to Interpol for a half-million-dollar reward. He seems to have no loyalties except to himself."

No 'honor among thieves' with Mr. Ra'd, huh?"

"You got it!" said Agent Alicia. "That's the picture Interpol paints?"

Allen tried again: "Where does he live? – if you can tell me?"

"About the best we can figure is all over the Caribbean. We have identified an estate in Cuba as one of his hangouts, or hideouts. There is even a luxurious estate in the mountains of the wretchedly poor country of Haiti. But Interpol says he seems to stay on the move and not stay anywhere very long."

"Interpol was a lot of help. This was a profitable trip then. Right?"

"Yes," said the FBI agent, "but let's not continue this quiz. Major Carlos will tell you all you need to know."

"Just one more question please, and it's not about this trip. Why is the FBI not sharing with other law enforcement agents all you know? For instance, the guy who murdered the custodian and the man pumping gasoline into the school boiler."

"I'll answer that 'one more' this way: if too many people know too much, the investigation is no longer confidential. Someone will talk. The confidential data goes to the wrong ears and corrupts the process. The criminals have ears, too. Information is their prized commodity. We keep some information out of the larger loop to keep it confidential. That also helps us find and plug leaks when the system gets leaky. Understand? Suppose you and I have a secret, and it gets out, and I know I did not tell it, who does that leave?"

"OK. I understand," said Allen. "Thanks for helping me understand a lot of things! Are you married?"

She smiled and shook her head in the negative. Then she said, "I thought the quiz was over!"

"Yes, Ma'am." Allen returned to his seat one row back and on a window on the other side of the jet. He watched the puffy white clouds on his side slipping swiftly and silently under the jet. He wondered how this trip might change the investigation. Were they any closer to catching the bad guys? Especially Mr. Ra'd?

Chapter Twelve
Learning to Fly

A new surprise waited for both boys on Saturday morning. The parents had agreed to let Major Carlos Perez-Cruz take both boys on a trip to the airport. They went first to a fixed-base operation run by the major's old friend and former navy shipmate, C. O. "Ben" Franklin. He had a Cessna 172 Skyhawk gassed and ready for flight.

The major asked the boys, "How would you like to have your first lesson in learning to fly?" There response was predictably enthusiastic.

First Lesson

Lesson one began with learning to do a walk-around inspection of the airplane. "We start with the propeller. Make sure it is smooth and free from nicks or cracks." He ran his fingers over the leading edge of the prop to show the way.

Satisfied with the prop, he stepped to his left, which he called the *starboard side* of the plane. He showed them how to open the cowling and look at the motor. There they checked the oil level and looked around for any wires out of place, any sign of oil or other fluids that should not be there.

When each boy had a look and was satisfied, he showed them how to secure the cowling again. Then they inspected the right wing. "The front of the wing is called the *leading edge*; the back is the *trailing edge*. You can lift the *ailerons* and make sure they move freely. When this one is up, the one on the opposite wing should be down and vice versa. These help us in making a turn in the air."

He showed them where to draw a couple of ounces of fuel into a clear plastic cup. They looked to see if there was any accumulation of water that might have condensed and contaminated the fuel. The instructor asked, "Will water be at the top or bottom of the gasoline?" They were assured it would be at the bottom. "Gasoline is lighter than water and floats on water like oil."

On down the fuselage he led them to the *elevators* on the tail assembly and the *rudder* on the *horizontal stabilizer*. He explained how a stream of air will lift or lower the tail or move it left or right on command of controls at the hands and feet of the pilot. And so on around the left side, also called by navy flyers the *port* side. "Are you getting all this? There is a lot to learn to become a pilot." He gave them a quiz for review of terms learned so far. "Point to the *starboard aileron*." They both did so immediately. "Point to the *elevator*."

They did. They found without trouble the leading edge and trailing edge of wings and *elevators*, the *prop, cowling*, and *rudder*. Then he said, point to the "*Pitot tube?*"

Both boys looked at each other a bit puzzled. Then Juan asked cautiously, "Would that be this gadget sticking out of the leading edge of this wing?"

"Very good!" said his instructor-dad. "That is a devise invented early in the history of aviation by a Frenchmen named *Pitot* to measure the flow of air so you can have an airspeed indicator on your 'dashboard,' so-to-speak. It's better known as your *instrument panel.* The cover on the *Pitot tube* hopefully keeps insects from clogging it up. The cover is automatically opened by the wind when you get any speed." He showed them how the hinged cover moved when any pressure was applied to the protruding flap on the tiny tube.

The major concluded with naming the *landing gear*, gently kicking a tire to check inflation, and pulling away from the landing gear tire a pairs of painted boards linked together by about twelve inches of rope. He sent Juan to do the same for the nose wheel and the port side landing gear. A more sturdy rope tied each wing to an anchor in the asphalt. These they loosed also as they finished their walk-around inspection.

Airborne

He showed them how to use the step to enter the airplane's *cabin*. Allen started in the back seat and Juan sat up front with the pilot. Here they were introduced to the pre-flight checklist, the gauges on the panel, the rudder controls, aileron controls, and radio. A label gave them the frequency for local ground control and tower.

"Clear!" called the major out the tiny window on his side. Then he turned the key starter to engage the propeller. It struggled a couple of turns then sprang to life. The pilot checked magnetos on *left, right* and *both.* He left it on the *"both"* setting for flying. He would explain this to the boys later. Closing the windows, he put on his earphones and handed another to Juan in the back seat. "Downtown Ground Control, this is Fiver-three Tango at Franklin Aviation. Directions and clearance to the active runway for local orientation flight."

The speaker barked back: "Fiver-three Tango, cleared to runway One Seven. Straight ahead to the taxiway, left to the active runway. There is one departure ahead of you. Contact the tower at One Niner Zero Point Fiver. Good day. "

The pilot answered, "Fiver-Three Tango. Thank you." He advanced the throttle to start rolling and backed off the throttle as the plane responded. He kept it idle speed so that the plane moved forward at a walking pace. He looked ahead and to each side and explained to the boys, "You need to 'rubberneck' a lot on the ground as well as in the air." As he neared the turn onto the active runway, he turned the radio knob to the frequency for the tower. The plane ahead of them was rolling down the runway for liftoff.

The major reached the end of the taxiway at runway 14.

He turned the plane into the wind and told the boys it was time to check the *magnetos.* "We set the breaks and hold the wheel back to keep the plane on the ground," he explained, "The *magnetos* are labeled *"Left, Both,* and R*ight.* We will run up the engine to about 1,000 rpm. Then we check each of three positions by listening and watching for any rough running. Normally, we fly on both, but if we have ignition trouble aloft, we can come home on one setting if we know which one is good." He checked each setting in order, and when he had reduced the throttle again to idle, he asked his students if everything sounded normal to them."

They guessed so. He smiled. "Assurance will come with experience. We are ready to go. He once again checked the controls: rudder, ailerons, brakes and all. "We are going to use a bit of flaps for easier lift off at low speed. Watch the trailing edge of the wings as I lower the flaps." Then glancing at each student, he asked, "Everybody ready?"

The major spoke to the control tower next, "Downtown Tower, Fiver Three Tango, ready for takeoff. "

The tower answered: "Fiver Three Tango, cleared for takeoff. Departure to the practice area cleared for downwind leg at approximately 360 degrees." He responded with a single click of his microphone button as he eased forward the throttle to turn onto the active runway and line up with the middle stripe. He advanced the throttle to *full throttle.* The plane surged down the middle of the runway.

The major shouted over the engine noise to explain to the boys, "We keep the plane straight with the rudder pedals at our feet. When we reach takeoff speed, about 60-65 knots ... (He put a finger on the air-speed indicator), the plane will want to fly. We will ease back on the yoke and lift her smoothly into the air." As predicted, they saw the runway receding under them. After two left turns, they left the flight pattern of the airport toward the rural land up the Red River.

The boys looked down at cotton fields brown now and busy with big green cotton-picking machines. And they saw row after row of green plants in the rich river bottomland. "What are they growing down there?" Juan wanted to know. The brown crop with white dots you maybe can't see from this distance is cotton. The green rows are soybeans. The cotton is brown now because it has been sprayed with a defoliate to make it easier for picking. The green row crop is soybeans. "

Over those fields the pilot gave orientation on straight and level flying, slow turns, climbing and gliding. After gaining altitude of a couple of thousand feet, they practiced slow flight and stalls. "We need to learn how slow the plane will fly before it stalls and falls out of the sky. And when it does stall, we need to know how to recover. We let the nose drop forward and add power to gain flying speed and flight control. Notice how sloppy and unresponsive the controls are at slow speed."

He asked Juan, "Do you think you can do that? Put your hand on the wheel. Put your other hand on the throttle.

Gently pull it back a little. The engine slows. Push the throttle gently forward. Notice the plane wants to climb."

Juan followed each instruction. He was flying the airplane! His instructor asked, "Now what will happen when you pull the yoke back?"

Juan answered, "We will go up?"

"Try it, gently." He did so. His dad pointed at the altimeter. "Did we gain altitude?"

"Not really," Juan answered.

"It is crucial to know that *altitude* is determined by the throttle; *attitude* of the plane is controlled by the *stick*, in this case the "stick" is a wheel or *yoke*. If you reduce gasoline to the engine by pulling back on the throttle, the plane will go down. If you give it the gas, we will climb even without pointing the nose upward. Don't try to control altitude by the yoke." He looked back to Allen, "Are you following all this?"

"I think so."

"We are going back to the airport and practice a couple of *touch-and-goes*. Then you will have your turn at hands-on flying in the front seat."

For practice landings they contacted the control tower for permission to do a few touch-and-go landings. There was no competing traffic, so permission was granted. They entered the flight pattern at 600 feet above the ground. That was about 800 feet on the altimeter; Downtown airport is almost 200 feet above sea level.

The major requested of the tower a straight-in approach for the first touch-and-go. It was granted. The pilot pointed out the "14" on the end of the runway they were approaching. "What does that mean?"

Juan said, "That's the number of the runway."

"Yes, said the instructor. But why don't they just name them One, Two, Three and Four?" with no answer offered, he explained, "The 14 indicates a compass heading of one-four-zero degrees. The compliment of that on the other end is 320 degrees or almost due north, 360 degrees. The prevailing winds in this part of the country are north and south, so that's the main runway."

The major touched down smoothly just past the "14" numbers. He kept it straight with his pedals as he slowed down. Then he gave it full power and soon lifted off again. After two left turns, he explained they were now flying downwind; that means the wind is behind them. Then they would need to make two left turns to come in for another landing. He pulled on a control knob marked *carburetor heat* but did not explain himself at that time.

He said, "We will maintain pattern altitude until we get directly opposite the place we want to touch down. Imagine an "X" about a hundred feet or so down the runway past the number. That is our target for touching down. When we are opposite the runway numbers, we will throttle back and lower the nose into a normal glade as we just practiced." The major did so at the proper time with Juan following through on the controls with hands and feet.

"Notice we are losing altitude but still have good flying speed. This is a *normal glide*. By practice you will learn what a *normal glide* feels like and looks like. We will extend the downwind leg a bit before we make our first left turn. We want the pattern to be clear to all who may see us. After a smooth left turn, he continued, "Now we are flying perpendicular to the runway; this is called the *base leg. Downwind, base leg*, and one more turn to line up with the runway for *final approach.* Keep your feet lightly on the rudders to see what I am doing. Remember we dip the wing and use the rudder to turn. Are you with me?"

"Yes sir."

"And Allen?"

"Yes sir, I think."

"Now we continue to glide as we line up with the runway. If we are too high, we can reduce the throttle. If we are coming in too low, we give it a bit more gas. I like to do that momentarily anyway to clear the carburetor and keep it from icing up. Are we in line?"

"Looks good to me," said Juan.

"Now as we cross the threshold of the runway, we throttle back completely and let the plane level off just above the runway. It will want to settle down. We will hold it off as long as we have flying speed. We will keep it low and slow so we do not land with a bounce." He touched down smoothly using the rudder pedals to roll out straight down the runway.

Landing Practice

Then as planned, he closed the carburetor heat and gave

it full throttle. Keeping it straight, he gained flying speed and gently lifted it into the air again. They went around twice more. On the last landing, he said to Juan, "Now this will be a full stop landing, and I want you to do the landing. I'll follow you on all your controls."

He took the microphone and requested of the tower a full-stop landing. The control tower was giving him his full attention. Carlos gave Juan encouragement and positive reinforcement for everything he did right. He bounced a little on contact with the runway, but altogether it was a good landing and the major told him so.

The instructor turned the radio to "Ground Control" for instructions back to Franklin Aviation. They deplaned to take a break before starting out again with Allen at the controls. Assured that no one had airsickness, the major bought cold drinks for all, and they talked about their experience while resting and refreshing in the shade of a wing.

Full of Questions

Allen and Juan agreed that there was a lot to learn about flying. They thought learning to drive a car would be much easier. While they were taking their rest break, they asked questions and answered a few from their instructor.

"How long does it take to learn to fly?" They learned that FAA regulations require at least 40 hours of flying time for the basic pilot's license. Sixty hours is more realistic. A student pilot can qualify to fly solo in as little as five to seven hours. A student pilot is not allowed to take passengers and has other restrictions. He needs solo time to develop skills and build confidence.

"How much does an airplane cost?" They learned that a good used Cessna 172 Skyhawk such as they were flying today would cost close to a year's wages for a working man or woman. A new one would cost a great deal more.

"How long does it take to become a fighter pilot like you?"

The major told them that becoming a jet fighter pilot takes a good deal of training, but if a young man is accepted into military pilot training, such as the Marines Aviation program, he could learn all he needed to know as a guest of the service that trains him. "And training is an on-going way of life. You never stop learning, and you never stop training," said the major. "But there is nothing quite like flying a Super Hornet on and off the deck of an aircraft carrier."

Juan asked, "How long do you think it will it take for me to learn to fly by myself?"

"To solo you need at least five hours instruction and the instructor's approval. You will also need to get an FAA physician's examination showing that you are physically fit for flying. You also need to be at least 14 years old."

"Wow! You mean I can get a student pilot's license before I am old enough to drive a car?"

"That's right," said the major. "You have to be at least 16 years old before you can earn a private pilot's certificate, but you can solo with a student pilots ticket at age 14. A student pilot is not allowed to take passengers. The private pilot's certificate allows you to take passengers, but you can't charge for that service without a commercial rating. You can't give lessons without an instructor's rating.

Juan looked at Allen and said, "It looks like you will be a pilot before I will." Allen just gave him a big grin.

Allen's Lesson

When they were rested and refreshed, Juan disposed of the cold drink cans while the major led Allen through another walk-around inspection. Then all three boarded the Cessna again. This time Juan took his place in the back. Allen took the left seat up front. They went over the same drill for takeoff with Allen talking to ground control and the tower. His instructor prompted each exchange with when to speak and what to say.

In the practice area up river from Downtown Airport, they practiced again slow flight and stalls, climbs and glides and turns. Major Carlos took it down to 1,000 feet to demonstrate a skill they would begin to learn in the next lesson or two. He did "S" turns across a road." He told them, "Learning this maneuver will help you adjust for the wind direction and wind velocity in the landing pattern."

Then Allen had his drill with touch-and-go landings. The major demonstrated and then followed on the dual controls while the student tried to do the same. When they were done, they landed and taxied back to Franklin Aviation. Major Carlos checked in the Cessna to his friend, the owner, and gave him a note with the tachometer readings at the beginning and end of their time.

Then they drove over to the terminal where the major bought a logbook for each of the new student pilots. They sat in the lounge where they watched the instructor inscribe the name of each in his log. He showed them how he would keep the record of the date and duration of each flight. He recorded the lessons covered. "Orientation flight: inspection, takeoffs and landings. He abbreviated them to save space in the logbook. "TO&Ls," (for takeoffs and landings, for example.) He logged instruction in straight-and-level flight, climbs and glides, turns, and radio orientation.

"I'll get some instruction material so you can begin ground school," he told them. "There is a lot to learn. You will have a great advantage learning together. Much of what you learn will be a big help with your schoolwork; Geometry, Science, especially Weather, and lots of other things. You will need to learn FAA regulations, map reading, navigation, weather science, radio protocol, and lots more. Are you ready for this?" Both boys were emphatic in the affirmative!

The major took a back exit from the airport and explained: "The day may come when you two will find the highways closed and you will need to get out of town. If I am deployed or otherwise not around, your mothers may drive you this route. I am going to seal some other instructions in an envelope at home with a copy in the airplane."

The boys looked at each other in puzzled response.

Chapter Thirteen
Esther is Missing

On a Friday evening, the boys were together at Allen's house trying to divide their attention between homework and computer games. Esther was enjoying a youth function at the church of one of her best girlfriends. Allen caught the phone when it rang. It was the youth pastor at the church where Esther was.

"Let me speak to your mother or dad immediately. This is Pastor Dave." Allen's dad was closest and was called to take the urgent phone call.

"Mr. Anderson, this is Pastor Dave. Esther's friend Ruthie just saw a man throw Esther into a white van and speed away. Ruthie is calling 911 at the minute on her cell phone. I'm going to get one of my helpers to watch the youth at our Bible study, and I'm going to see if I can pick up their trail. I'll be in touch!"

As soon as Mr. Anderson hung up, his wife was standing near, summoned by the urgent tone in the questions from her husband. He told her what little he had just learned. Then he picked up the phone and called Deputy Newton. The deputy said he would get out an Amber Alert immediately for the van and Esther but wanted to know more details. "Did anyone get a license plate number? Even what state issued the license? Any distinguishing marks on the van? Anything at all? ... OK, we will have to go with what we have, but do you have any idea how many white vans are on the road even at night? We are looking for a commercial-type white van, no windows as in a passenger van. Right? See if you can get a description of the man who abducted her from Ruthie or any other witness. I think I will need to call our FBI contact on this, too."

The Online Search

Allen had started searching online as soon as he heard what his dad said about Esther abducted. He went to a *Find-my-Phone* website and signed in. He entered Esther's cell phone number and her ID number. By the time his dad was off the phone, he had Esther's phone located on a map. "Got her!" he shouted. "She's northbound on Interstate 49 approaching the I-20 interchange." Everyone gathered around the computer screen and watched as the tiny light made the westbound swing on I-20. They seemed to be traveling at a high rate of speed.

"Maybe they will draw the attention of a police cruiser!" said Esther's dad. "Oh God, please help us!" He picked up the house phone and tried Deputy Newton again. He was disappointed but not surprised at the persistent busy signal. Mrs. Anderson knew the number of the sheriff's department by heart and dictated it to her husband. Tell someone that this is an emergency. If Mr. Newton is at the office, they can interrupt him."

Meanwhile, Juan was using his cell phone to dial their FBI contacts. Neither one was on duty this evening or at all available. Juan insisted that this was a life-and-death emergency and he needed help now! It seemed like a long wait, but another agent picked up on the call. "What's this life-and-death emergency?" he asked casually.

Juan answered in his matter-of-fact tone: "My friend Allen Anderson and I have been helping the FBI and others track down and apprehend a terrorist who tried to firebomb our school during a public meeting. A few minutes ago, Allen's sister was kidnapped from a church youth rally and hauled away in a white van. We have tracked her cellphone online and are watching it speed west on I-20 at the moment. It's time for authorities to get on this now, don't you think?"

"Hold on just a minute!" said the FBI agent.

About that time, Allen's house phone rang. It was Deputy Newton again. Mr. Anderson, eyes still bonded to the computer screen, told the deputy what they were witnessing. "They are westbound still and now passing the State Fairgrounds. This is an amazing website!" The deputy asked if Allen could give him the URL address and stay online to guide him through the connection to Esther's phone. While he was doing so, the FBI came back on the line with Juan.

Mr. Matter-of-Fact Juan repeated the agent's most recent communication back to him: "Hold on just a minute." Everyone in the room could hear the agent's loud objection to this turn of events.

The FBI was not organized for hot pursuit, and at the moment the Sheriff's Department did not have a car on the west side of the parish. They tried to coordinate with city police and state police who were now getting the Amber Alert.

Juan let the FBI officer stew a minute and then he brought him up-to-the minute with the abduction, Amber Alert, online search and current location of Esther's cell phone, presumably still in her pocket in the westward speeding white van. Juan offered an opinion, for what it might be worth to the FBI. "This has to be the work of that same cold-blooded killer we are calling *Mr. A.* Maybe this time his henchmen will lead the police right to him." Juan pushed the speaker button on the phone so that Allen and his parents could hear both ends of the conversation. He noted to the agent that it had been only about 15 minutes since the abduction took place.

Texas Rangers Join the Chase

Deputy Newton called Major Carlos and told him he was going to also call the Harrison County Texas Sheriff's office to bring them into the search. Major Carlos urgently requested that the Texas deputies not try to apprehend or at all confront the white van but keep them under surveillance only. "I'm at

Barksdale Air Force Base. We can have a professional SWAT team ready to helicopter to wherever they stop." Deputy Newton agreed.

While they were talking, the website indicated the target was taking Exit 633 onto northbound rural Texas highway 134. They seemed to be slowly moving north toward Jonesville, the next intersection. Major Carlos ventured the judgment that being off the interstate "tells us that they are not going much further."

He added: "I'll have a drone tracking them in five minutes or no more than ten. They won't get away! We will welcome Harrison County Sheriff's eyes on the ground if they don't let themselves be seen and alert the culprits."

As they had done twice already, Allen and Juan walked Major Carlos and his office through the *Find-My-Phone* website. They soon had their target on another computer screen. Everyone followed as the pace slowed through several zigzags on other county roads. Juan kept his screen closing in on the target until they came to stop right in a barn behind a farmhouse.

"It looks like they are at their destination for the night, " suggested Major Carlos, and he gave a phone number to all on the phone. "This line will be open and dedicated to this operation as long as we need it. Pass the word to any other law enforcement agencies that this is HDQ for this abduction case. We will work with those who want to be involved, but they need to work through this office. We don't need different law agencies out there in the dark shooting at each other."

The Harrison County office soon reported that a mounted patrol would be mobilized and moved to the area north of the target. "They will be ready for rapid deployment in the woods when needed."

Ransom Note

Within a half hour, Esther's parents had a text message from her I-phone. But it was not Esther. The message was signed "Mr. A." That told them all that this bold fugitive somehow did have inside information about this investigation. And the slim possibility that this was an unrelated abduction was now out of the equation. The message said:

"Soon you will get a FedEx delivery with a lock of hair recently donated by your daughter Esther. She begs you to cooperate fully and swiftly with her hosts. We want you to be assured that this is not all about money. Our demands are:

First, the families of both boys and their parents will cease all communication and all cooperation with officers of the law, effective immediately. This communication is not to be shared with any of them.

Second, to defray our expenses so far, you will gather $5,000 in a variety of denominations, used U.S. currency, not in sequence of serial numbers and not marked at all. Instructions about where to leave the money will be in our next communication.

Third, I know you will be glad to see Esther walking into her home unharmed. I assure you, you will never see her at all ever again, if you do not obey these directives explicitly. We have the family under surveillance and will know if you contact anyone at all about this letter.

Fourth, if you are not fully convinced by the lock of hair, next time we can send you an index finger bearing her fingerprint and her favorite pink nail polish. If you are not prompt, other body parts will follow as long as she survives.

Fifth, Esther may decide that instead of donating body parts, she will put on the burka and convert to Islam and become the newest bride of a certain sheik in a faraway desert kingdom. I know that he will pay many gold coins endowment for such a beautiful young virgin with blond hair and blue eyes.

Of course, you care for your daughter. Now prove it by explicit obedience to my demands.

Sincerely,

"Mr. A"

The communication sent a cold shiver through all who read it. Yet to keep it secret was now out of the question; too many people already knew of the abduction. More than forty friends were at the church when it happened. By now they had spread the word to hundreds. The Amber Alert was telling thousands more, at least with such details as could be told at all. Law enforcement of all kinds was already on the case and now knew precisely where Esther was.

Soon the cell phone signal moved from the barn to the house. Esther might be in either place. The Barksdale team soon had a drone taking aerial photographs of that farm and its environment. Representatives of the FBI, the two sheriff's departments on each side of the Texas/Louisiana line, the state police of both states and others were sending representatives to Barksdale. Every one of them had to be carefully vetted at the gate. As soon as they were cleared, each was escorted to a room with two large viewing screens on the wall. There they could see in real time what was happening at the farm --- at least the bird's eye view.

The deputy from Harrison County, Texas soon recognized the farm and told all present that the place was vacant, boarded up, and listed for sale with a realtor. There will be "no cattle in the pasture or other animals beyond the two-legged kind." Several of the law-enforcement parties were forwarding every particle of data to their own offices by cell phone. The Barksdale moderator of this gathering stressed how important it was to keep TV and Radio media out of the information loop. "They can sure screw up a rescue operation."

Every piece of data was added to the mix. For instance, Esther's friend at the church who saw her abducted recalled that she saw the driver of the white van. When the side door was momentarily opened to throw Esther inside, the dome light was on. She described the driver as "an unshaven fat slob." The teen told the city police who came to the church to investigate that she felt sure she would recognize the driver if she ever saw him again. That no one could identify the white van better was now a non-issue.

The only two eyewitnesses were confident that there

were only two men in the van, the driver and the guy who snatched their victim.

Esther's parents composed a reply to the ransom message and read it to Deputy Newton who was in his patrol car approaching the Anderson home. The email for Esther's I-phone said.

Mr. A:

Of course, we want our daughter back unharmed and as soon as possible. This is Friday night; the banks are closed and will be closed until Monday morning. I can't get the cash you demand until then. Suppose I give you two gold coins worth $4,000 total and the rest in cash and silver bullion. I can get these with my credit card from a coin shop tomorrow morning (Saturday). We want Esther back unharmed and immediately."

(signed) Esther's Parents.

Deputy Newton thought the message was appropriate. They pressed the "send" button prayerfully and began the tense wait for an answer.

It took about ten minutes for a reply for some unknown reason, but the ringleader sent back:

"Dear Parents:

Your suggestion is acceptable except make it three Krugerrands plus $1,000 dollars in cash and silver bullion. Mostly cash. No more excuses!

Sincerely,

"Mr. A"

Mr. and Mrs. Anderson were willing to pay any price to get their daughter back unhurt, but they had reason to hope that the authorities would win this round. The wheels were already turning at Barksdale Air Force Base. Meanwhile it was to the advantage of the good guys for the bad guys to think that they were winning.

Chapter Fourteen
The Raid

The Anderson family realized that there was no way that the abduction could be kept a secret. Some forty people were at the youth fellowship when it happened. City police came and interviewed many of them. An Amber Alert had already been posted; the very perpetrators might even have seen the notice on the big highway sign near the state line. These were things they did not want to mention to the kidnappers, but the wheels were in motion for a rescue attempt anyway.

The SWAT Team

Major Carlos Perez-Cruz and his Air Force partner, Major Trevor Washington were agreed they needed to get boots on the ground. Major Carlos soon was briefing his SWAT team, and outfitting them for the mission. He showed them an aerial map of the layout of the farm. "This is our destination in Harrison County, Texas. We have just learned that the property is vacant, boarded up and listed for sale. We have a Boeing 160 Hummingbird drone over the target, watching and taking these pictures. We will approach through the piney woods north of the property. We then will cross this open field. It is overgrown pastureland. We want to keep the barn between the house and us. We have reason to believe at least two kidnappers are holed up in the farmhouse. The captive victim may be with them in the house, but we will clear the hay barn first on the way to the house. We know the white van used in the abduction is in the barn.

"The mastermind of this abduction we know is a cold-blooded killer. You need to assume that the kidnappers are just as deadly, but if possible we need to take them alive. We need their help in finding the kingpin. I will lead and penetrate the barn from the rear if possible. I will stay in touch with Major Trevor Washington's SWAT team waiting in the woods to the north of the pasture and the barn. Your headsets are preset to the frequency we will all be using. We will use night-vision goggles if the moonlight allows it. Try to avoid using any other light that might alert the farmhouse before we are ready to enter it.

"I know you are all sniper qualified, but the three with sniper rifles will play that role. The rest of us will be armed with assault rifles and .45 caliber automatics and your knife. We are going in as light as possible to be as fast as possible.

"Major Washington will lead the main body and deploy

resources as he sees fit. We will hop to the landing area. It is a small clearing about a kilometer north of the barn and farmhouse." He was designating the points on the map with a laser pointer. "We will drop down in two helicopters; there is room for only one at a time to unload. They are ready on the flight line at the moment. Any questions?"

One member of the team asked: "Do they know we are coming?"

"They would have to be stupid not to suspect it, but evidence available so far makes us believe they may be stupid. Even so, we will exercise every reasonable precaution. You know, "stupid" is more unpredictable and therefore often more dangerous. We need this to be a complete surprise to the bad guys. Take care of yourself and each other. No mistakes, no casualties!

"Our helicopter hop will take only about ten minutes. That will be time enough to apply nighttime grease to our faces. The crescent moon will be up about 30 degrees and slightly over the house target. When we are not in the shadow of the barn or the farmhouse, we will be moving almost directly into the moon. Expect a mostly unclouded sky. We should be in and out in fifteen minutes or so, if all goes well."

The Assault

The team was at the landing zone in about 10 minutes as predicted. They were gratified to see a state police car with his spotlight and his flashlight giving some illumination to an otherwise dark clearing. The two whirlybirds dipped to the ground in order as planned just long enough for the SWAT team to hit the ground and clear the zone. Then the whirlybirds were up and away to a bigger clearing to await the call to return.

Major Carlos led them through the woods. Another break for the good guys was a recent logging road through the forty acres of pines recently selectively harvested.

They gained the clearing in a matter of minutes. There they spread out and took cover behind the barbwire fence in the brush of the fence line.

Major Carlos asked his partner, Major Washington, to check the team to see that everyone was in place and ready. Major Carlos glanced at the moon and made a dash for the cover of the dark shade of the barn. There he took a prone position and adjusted his night-vision goggles to survey the situation. He asked his Air Force teammate to join him in this position. He soon had his partner in a similar position about ten yards to his right but still in the shadow of the barn. He signaled for Major Washington to hold his position while he made a dash to the barn.

Suddenly a hound across the road from the farmhouse seemed to catch their scent or otherwise know they were near. He began a persistent bark. Major Washington told the main body of the team to hold their positions. He added, "We are advancing to the barn." He saw Major Carlos point at him and wave him on to the barn position."

There, Major Carlos found the backdoor nailed shut.

The Stranger in Medallion Loafers

He did find one vertical plank loose at the bottom enough for him to pull it up and swing it to the side. He needed a second board to make an entrance large enough for the men to squeeze through in their bulletproof vests. With the two majors working together, they soon had that opening. One after the other slipped inside.

Before them was the white van. They soon determined it was unoccupied. The keys were not to be found. Major Carlos, with his penlight, read the VIN number from the dashboard to his communication officer. Then he did the same for the Texas license number, the make and model. He asked the communication officer to forward it on to the home base and see if they could identify anyone belonging to it. It looked for all the world to Major Carlos that it was a rental.

Just then Major Washington motioned that there was someone in the hayloft overhead. Major Washington backed off for maximum view of the loft with assault rifle ready. Major Carlos shouldered his assault rifle and started up the ladder to the loft. He could hear someone moving around in the hay.

"Before he raised his head over the last rung of the ladder, he called in a soft voice, "Esther, is that you?"

The Rescue

"Umm! Umm! Umm!" she answered. And thump, thump went her heels on the hay-lined loft. In three quick steps, the major was up the ladder. In two or three strides he was

121

to Esther. A flash of his penlight showed her trussed up in silver duct tape around her eyes, her mouth, her ankles and her wrists.

With a gentle touch of his sharp assault knife, the major cleared her mouth first, then her eyes, her wrists, and before he could get her ankles cleared she was wrapping both arms around his neck. "I knew you would come! I knew it! I've been praying for you to find me!"

"And we have been praying for you too. The boys tracked your journey from the church to here with an online website tracing your cellphone." He turned to his partner and suggested he bring the rest of the team in this far. He had lots of questions for Esther but he limited them to two themes: "Did they hurt you? How many are in the house?"

Esther said they did not hurt her at all except in tossing her around in the van to tape her up." She told Carlos that "the boss" was here waiting for them. She did not see him but heard him reminding the thugs not to hurt "the package." She said: "But I think he drove away in a car shortly after all three of them left me here."

"They are so stupid!" she suggested. "They taped my arms behind me at the wrist. Don't they know that a girl can pull her arms around her feet and get her hands and arms in front? I've been working on getting my eyes uncovered and my mouth cleared. But I was afraid if they came back and found I could see them, they might kill me. I wanted to get all the tape off and run away, but ... " The tears would hold no longer. "But I don't know where we are and had no idea which way to run! I asked God to lead you to find me! He did!" Her arms were still around his neck as he finished clearing tape from her ankles. The other team members began to squeeze through the opening and assemble inside except for two with sniper rifles who were positioned at corners of the barn with a view of the farmhouse. The lone hound was still barking occasionally, and a distant neighbor's dog began to answer.

Major Carlos helped Esther down the ladder and took off his bulletproof vest and put it on her. He pointed to a female member of the SWAT team to come forward and take charge of Esther. "As soon as you have the circulation back in your legs so you can run, " Major Carlos whispered, "Sgt. Beverly here is going to take you across the back pasture and through the woods to a drop zone where a helicopter will pick you up and take you to Barksdale Base Hospital for a good checkup. Your mother will probably be there by the time you are."

He looked at the Communications officer who nodded and began to relay the message. When the sergeant and Esther were out the back opening, Major Carlos whispered to his partner. "What's the best way to assault the house?"

Major Washington answered. "With that persistent dog in the equation, I would hold the team in this position while you and I take the next objective. If the team hears gunfire, they can come on the run. If our luck holds out this good, we will catch them sleeping in spite of the dog."

Luck or Providence, they found the back door lock already broken by the intruders. Major Carlos crept around the house using a stethoscope to listen for sounds from inside.

When he got back to the backdoor, he smiled at his partner. "I hear two men snoring. That's all. Let's go in."

The back screen door was old and squeaky, but they both made it inside with no issues. They were in the kitchen. Both men could smell alcohol and barbecue. Major Carlos wrinkled up his nose and looked at his partner through night-vision goggles. Washington whispered, "That's rum in one and whiskey in the other." They scanned the kitchen and found a sack with barbecue sandwiches for more than one meal. There were pork rib bones in the sink.

Major Carlos noted the species and decided, *At least one of them is not an observant Muslim. Probably both.* When they had surveyed the room, Major Carlos flipped up his night vision goggles to grow accustomed to the darkness before advancing to the front room where a small candle or lantern was giving a night light to the two sleeping drunks.

Major Washington did likewise. When Washington nodded ready, Major Carlos slipped through the opening and stepped to the left. His partner slipped in and stepped to the right. Both targets seemed to be still asleep on air mattresses in opposite corners of the otherwise bare floor. The one on his side was no longer snoring but was still breathing slow and heavy. The majors looked around the room. There was an opening to their left, which Major Carlos soon determined to be a hallway to one other empty room and a primitive bathroom. Major Carlos soon cleared them and returned to the room with the sleeping men. He quietly advanced on one and his partner the other. They slowly pressed the muzzle of their assault rifle into the ear of the one on his side and to the nose of the snoring fat fellow.

The kidnappers were not swift in coming out of their stupor. The one on his back swatted at the presence on his nose and soon was awake enough to know what it was. The other one reached for a weapon and heard Major Carlos warn him. "If you touch that pistol, I will scatter your brains. The Marines have landed and the Air Force, too. "

Soon both prisoners were sitting up, rubbing their eyes or otherwise trying to grasp the reality. The hound across the street was still sounding his persistent alert.

Major Carlos held his weapon on them while Major Washington rolled over each prisoner in turn and secured them with nylon cable ties for handcuffs. Then he began to search the room for weapons, for Esther's cellphone and any other important items. He soon found the cell phones. The major spoke to them both: "I assume you speak English when you are more sober. I could read you your rights, but I want you to know that you don't have any rights except such as may apply to prisoners of war. What do you have to say?"

One gruffly replied, "I want to see my lawyer!" Both military men looked at each other and laughed out loud. They were much more relaxed now.

Mayor Washington touched his microphone and informed the team: "We have two suspects in custody and the house is cleared. Keep the perimeter posted, but send the cameraman in and the Communications officer. Others may come in if you like."

While the photographer was recording the scene in video and digital stills, the communications officers sent word to the Barksdale situation room for those assembled to know the operation was successful with no casualties. Major Carlos added: "The kingpin is still not in custody. We are going to leave two or three here in the farmhouse in case he returns. He may have just gone to send a Fed-Ex to the Anderson address. Stress to all involved that there can be no public announcement while the number one suspect is still at large! None whatsoever! Be clear about that!"

"Let me know when Esther arrives safely at the base hospital, and when her mother is there to be with her." He soon got an affirmative reply to both those queries.

To Major Washington, he asked, "Who would you like to leave at this location? And where would you post them? Inside?"

The Air Force major answered: "I have two volunteers. They will clear the attic before we leave. They may get into the barbecue sandwiches when we are gone, but there is no liquor remaining." This last he offered with a wry smile and wide eyes that spoke volumes.

The team retreated as unobtrusively as they entered and followed Major Washington across the pasture, dragging and pushing their two reluctant and still drunken prisoners through the pine thicket. They arrived to the landing zone where the two helicopters soon picked them all up for the return to Barksdale.

Chapter Fifteen
The End of the Line?

October was inviting November to come spread even more colorful pigments on the canvas of fall foliage. A brisk breeze was pulling leaves from the trees already gold and purple and every shade of green and yellow and sending them fluttering in glorious display. In the middle of the afternoon, Esther's parents were at the kitchen table in the bay window enjoying the fall display and coffee. Esther came into the kitchen: "I have an idea!" They turned their attention to her. "Let's have a barbecue for Major Carlos and his family *and* his SWAT team!"

The parents looked at each other and then at Esther. "That's a wonderful idea!" said her mother. "Let's do it!" said her father. "Could we pull it together by this Saturday?"

Planning the Barbecue

Mrs. Anderson answered her husband: "You plan the

menu, and I'll work on the guest list."

Mr. Anderson said, "I like the idea of barbecue, baked beans and potato salad. I can fire up the outside grill, but we may need to cater some of it or pick up ribs at "Old Smokey's Bar-B-Q." Esther can help with boiling and peeling a six-pound bag of potatoes for potato salad. I'll start a grocery list."

Mrs. Anderson said, "I'll call Juanita and Carlos and get started on the guest list. Better yet, I'll call and ask if I can come over and get her advise and input on the plans!" Mrs. Anderson picked up her cell phone and called Juanita. She was soon out the door still talking to her neighbor on the way next door. When she came back twenty minutes later, she said, "You better make that bag of potatoes at least eight pounds. The guest list is growing. We will invite about twenty or twenty-five from Barksdale. We don't want to leave anyone out! Then we need to invite our FBI and Sheriff's department contacts. We certainly want to include Tom Newton and those of his deputy staff who guarded our place on some long nights. And we need to think about inviting a few of the close neighbors who have been so patient with our crisis? We should plan to feed thirty or forty people!"

"I'll help," said Esther, "I can make a big batch of Coleslaw, and I'm sure Allen and Juan will help, too. They can help keep the kitchen clean and help serve everyone. Allen will want at least a case of root beer on the menu. "

Mrs. Anderson said, "Oh, yes! And Juanita wants to help with the food. She will bake cakes and brownies for everyone.

You guys can decide on what to drink. Juanita has a big cooler for iced tea and a couple of big ice chests for canned drinks. And they offered to help buy the groceries! We are on a roll. "

Mr. Ra'd and Texas Rangers

That evening, Major Carlos spent a lot of time taking a couple of calls on his cell phone. He told Juanita that he would need to leave about 5:00 AM the next morning and might be gone a couple of days. He promised to call if it looked as if he might not be back for the Saturday gathering.

His Barksdale partner told him he sent a jeep to pick up the two members of the SWAT team after two days of waiting in the farmhouse with no return of the kingpin at all. He also told him that The Texas Rangers had tried to round up Senior Ra'd with no success. The kidnapper tried without success to collect the ransom money from a couple posing as the Andersons. He had them bring the gold and silver coins and followed them on I-20 westbound. He told them when to slow down and kept them reducing speed until they were at a crawl. Then he had them open the passenger-side window and on his cell-phone command, toss the zippered moneybag out the window. Then he commanded them to resume speed and not look back.

He planned it so the paying couple would soon be over a hill and out of sight of the drop zone. He had a confederate in a following car to snatch the bag and make a U-turn to the near exit eastbound. That exit was a north/south rural road that connected the Interstate to old Highway 80 running parallel to the interstate. At this point "Old 80" was about ten miles north of the Interstate. On this connecting road, his confederate was apparently instructed to pull into the parking lot of a certain Baptist church and put the moneybag in the large mailbox near the front door of the unoccupied church.

An 18-wheeler was waiting beside the church to pick up the package and take it to Mr. Ra'd at a truck stop a few miles away. All went well until the trucker pulled into the truck stop and went into the restaurant to deliver the bag to its destination. The kidnapper saw the Texas Rangers come speeding into the parking lot of the truck stop. Three Rangers jumped out and headed for the trucker. Mr. Ra'd casually but immediately made his exit out the back door and over a fence to where his car waited. The drop proved to be a sack of pennies. The Trucker was taken into custody but did not know enough to provide any helpful information. He identified the man who hired him for this little chore by one of his wanted pictures as our Mr. Ra'd.

Interpol Calling

The news Major Carlos shared with Major Washington was a call from their Interpol friends. Ra'd had been spotted returning to the Caribbean. He was reported to be now at his villa in the mountains of Cuba. There he had a wife and children. Interpol had reason to believe he also had another wife in a secure villa in the highlands of Haiti. And they had unconfirmed information about at least one more wife and family on another island hideaway in the Bahamas.

Majors Carlos and Washington took their Barksdale corporate Learjet to Miami. Staff had arranged to hanger it there. There they had prearranged for a Cessna 310 twin engine to fly to Cuba and wherever else they needed to go to find Mr. Ra'd.

Their Interpol connection met them in Cuba where they visited the Imam of a Mosque. The Imam told them, "Yes, I know Senior Ra'd. He is well known here. He occasionally visits our mosque in efforts to recruit young men for Jihad. But he is not one of us, and that also is well known. He does not keep the Seven Pillars of Islam. He does not know the Koran or answer the calls to prayer.

"He hates Americans, of course, but that hatred is not driven by his religion if he has any! I don't believe he does. "

The majors often asked why he hates America but got no more than a shrug for an answer from anyone.

They confirmed from two other sources, that Ra'd only attends prayers when he is on the prowl for some manpower. He spreads money around and talks big, but he is known to be a man to avoid.

In three other official visits arranged by their Interpol connection, they heard similar reports. The Cuban Police told Interpol that the Mafia wanted to kill Ra'd as much as the Americans want to capture him. He has cheated them more than once. He runs drugs for them to Florida, but recently he paid for a big shipment with counterfeit US bills. Then he brokered a big shipment for a steamer going from the Dominican Republic to Europe. After he got his money, he sold out the smugglers to Interpol for reward money. He's on everyone's Most Wanted list including the Mafia.

While they were making their rounds, the Interpol friend got a call from his office. R'ad had filed a flight plan in a twin-engine Piper PA-23 Aztec that he was going to fly from San Juan, Puerto Rico across the Bahamas to Jacksonville, Florida.

Major Washington asked, "When are they leaving, and when do they arrive?"

"The first thing you need to know," said the Interpol officer, "is that R'ad never files flight plans. He doesn't want authorities to be able to know any of his business, especially any of his coming and going into the States. But he does this time? I smell a rat!"

Major Carlos asked, "That rat maybe smell like a Piper Aztec lost at sea in the Bermuda Triangle?"

"Precisely!" said his Interpol connection. "When a criminal has too many people closing in on him to arrest him or to kill him, he suddenly fakes his death and goes into deep hiding! I think we are about to lose the trail of our Senior R'ad. I'll try to get ahead of the search and have our people check with anyone we know, to see what we can find out. Maybe one of his known wives went with him. If not, when do they expect him back?"

Major Carlos said he would alert the coast guard of the flight plan and the suspicion that the plane has a planned disappearance somewhere in the Bahamas. With this breaking news of their rabbit, the hounds decided to head for home. By the time they got to Miami, R'ad's Piper had already disappeared from radar. There was no way to know if he was flying under radar and might have changed course or continued over the Bahamas. He could have landed at one of many airports close to his planned track. By the time the majors were back at Barksdale about midnight, the Piper was officially declared lost. The Coast Guard was mounting a search and planning for the Civil Air Patrol to be organized for a more thorough search beginning at sunup.

Major Carlos went home and left Major Washington to post a watch to garner any news as it came in. If any urgent news broke, their sleep could be interrupted. There was no news from the Coast Guard or Interpol or the FAA or anyone. It seemed that the slippery Mr. R'ad had given them the big slip this time.

The Party

At 5:00 PM the guests began to arrive and make their way to the Anderson's backyard where the aroma of barbeque was drawing a crowd. In time for the 6:00 PM serving, two long folding tables end-to-end and covered with real fabric tablecloths were in place in the back yard. The ladies soon had them spread with everything it takes to make a sumptuous Louisiana barbeque.

Mrs. Anderson used a cast iron pot lid and a big serving

spoon to announce the call to dinner. She introduced her husband to give a few words of welcome and instructions for self-service and to lead in a prayer of blessing of the food and of these gathered friends.

Mr. Anderson stepped up to the table and noted there is

plenty of food and no one should be bashful. He said, "There are hot dogs and spicy sausage on the grill and barbecue chicken." He promised to be there to help the youngsters. "Brisket and barbecue chicken and pork ribs are on the table. We have a mountain of potato salad, hot buttered rolls, Coleslaw, and a dish my wife calls 'Man-pleasing Baked Beans.' Everybody will love 'em.

"We thank God for every one of you, and we offer this

gathering as a token of our thanks. Let's pray God's blessing on it all." Then he bowed and invoked the favor of the Almighty on this food, these friends, and this fellowship. When he had said "Amen," he gestured to the table and said, "Enjoy!"

Question and Answer Time

The fall evening faded into darkness and the fire pit reduced to glowing embers. A few children were roasting marshmallows. Most guests began to crowd into the den where someone was playing the piano. Esther wanted to gather the SWAT team for a group photo. Small groups all evening had tended to gather around Majors Carlos and Washington. The two leaders tended to defer to each other with no hint of inter-service rivalry. Since the two boys and their families were now well known to the terrorist, there was little reason for the secrecy that had kept information in a tight circle.

Soon the two majors now in civilian sportswear were standing shoulder-to-shoulder fielding questions from the guests. *What happened to Mr. Ra'd?*

Major Washington brought them up to the minute with their trip yesterday to the Caribbean and the report of "lost at sea somewhere in the Bermuda Triangle – or maybe not." The men assured everyone that the kingpin would remain on the Ten Most Wanted List of the FBI and Interpol. And Tom Newton added, "And the Caddo Parish Sheriff's Department, too!"

Mr. Anderson took that as a good time to express undying gratitude to the men who stood watch many nights in the back yard with mosquitos and other pests.

"What can you tell us about Esther's kidnapping?" They deferred to Esther herself for that one. She related her abduction and the eerie sounds of the hayloft and the duct tape over eyes and mouth and wrists and ankles. She told of the overwhelming joy and relief when the SWAT team found her and spirited her away to the waiting helicopter.

Someone wanted to hear from the boys about how they became involved in this adventure from the beginning. Allen and Juan took turns telling of the first sighting of the terrorist setting a bomb to blow up their school with public officials and a public assembly in the auditorium. Juan told of witnessing the murder of the school custodian who was in cahoots with the terrorist and then betrayed by him.

Juan took the occasion for a public thanks to his best friend, Allen, for helping him through so many tense times. He mentioned once when Allen helped him settle his fear about dying so young and without assurance of eternal salvation.

Major Washington ducked out to take a cell-phone message from his office. When he returned he told everyone he had just learned that the Civil Air Patrol might have spotted some pieces of the wreckage of R'ad's plane that disappeared at sea. The Coast Guard sent a cutter to the location to check it out.

"How incredibly convenient!" remarked Major Carlos

sardonically.

"Yes," added Major Washington, "maybe just a bit too convenient and a bit too incredible to believe. Believe me, we will find Mr. R'ad dead or alive, in the water or in hiding!"

Just then, Esther's camera flashed on the group of SWAT team members. Mrs. Anderson and Juanita both startled, looked at each other, and then looked around to see if someone were taking a picture of their children. Then the mothers looked again at each other and had a good laugh.

Three days later Major Carlos had a cable from Interpol at his Barksdale office. It reported on their investigation of the last flight of Mr. R'ad. First, evidence from the site of the plane crash in the southern zone of the Bermuda triangle indicated an intentional crash landing at sea. A cigar boat from Cuba waited in the crash zone to rescue the pilot.

Second, Interpol agents, with the help of Cuban authorities talked to one of the men waiting in the cigar boat. They reported their reason for being at the crash sight and claimed that the plan was unsuccessful because of a hard landing of the heavy plane, breaking up and sinking swiftly with pilot still in it. They waited a while and looked around to see if he would surface with the inflatable life vest he was reported to be wearing. They say he never surfaced (and they complained about not being paid for their trip from Cuba and back). Though R'ad was a licensed pilot and rated for the twin-engine land aircraft, he was not a very experienced pilot.

Third, the Woods Hole Oceanographic Institute found the

wreck in 400 feet of water with their deep-water explorer. Photographic evidence and samples retrieved proved conclusively that Mr. R'ad perished in the crash. He was still buckled into the pilot's seat with his life vest yet to be inflated. The body has not yet been recovered.

One item retrieved by the explorer was a pair of Amico medallion loafers doubled bagged in plastic bags.

Left to right: Esther Anderson with her parents. Then, Major Carlos with Juan and Juanita (his son and his wife). Seated: Allen Anderson. The stray dog is unidentified.

www.ingramcontent.com/pod-product-compliance
Lightning Source LLC
Chambersburg PA
CBHW071810090426
42737CB00012B/2023